Beaded Jewelry

with
Found Objects

*Incorporate Anything
from Buttons to Shells*

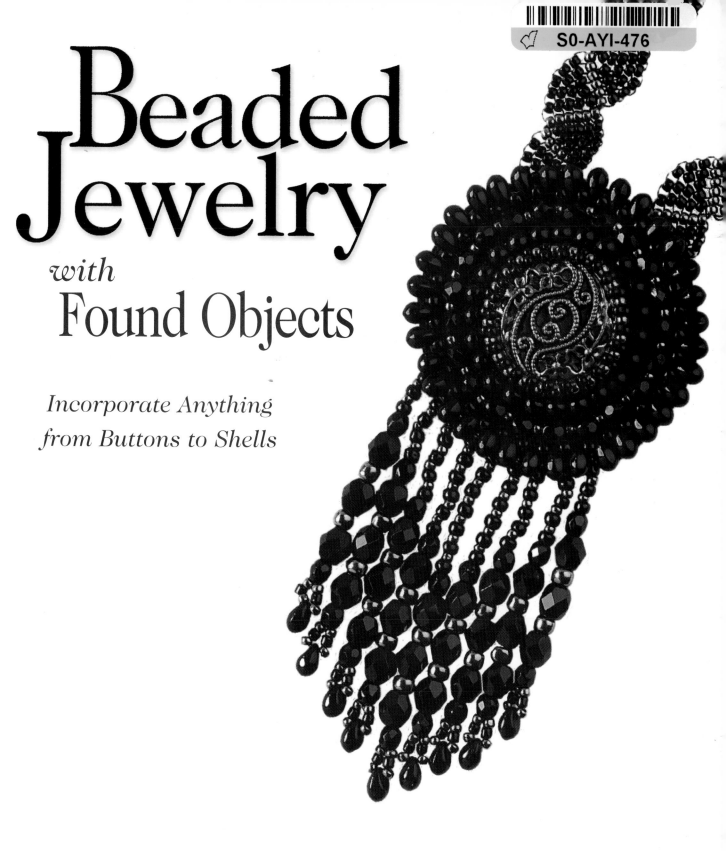

Carole Rodgers

Published by

krause publications
An F&W Publications Company

700 East State Street • Iola, WI 54990-0001
715-445-2214 • 888-457-2873
www.krause.com

Please call or write for our free catalog of publications. Our toll-free number
to place an order or obtain a free catalog is (800) 258-0929.

Library of Congress Catalog Number: 2003115886

ISBN: 0-87349-684-1

Edited by Maria L. Turner

Designed by Jamie M. Griffin

DEDICATION

For LeRoy, my husband, best friend, and No. 1 fan. Thank you for your support. Without you, this book would never have been written. I love you.

ACKNOWLEDGMENTS

I am truly grateful to the generous and innovative ladies who let me use photographs of their work in these pages. Their full biographies, including which pieces they submitted, are located in the back of the book, page 127. I also appreciate those who shared their knowledge of beading with me and with all of you, the readers. Thank you all so much.

I wish to thank the following companies for their help as well:

Azotic Coating Technology, Inc.

Beacon Adhesives

Beadalon

Making Tracks, Ink.

Morning Light Emporium

One-of-a-Kind Rock Shop

Wild Things Beads

Lastly, I wish to thank the people at Krause Publications for making this book happen: editor Maria Turner, page designer Jamie Griffin, cover designer Marilyn McGrane, photographer Kris Kandler, and acquisitions editor Julie Stephani.

TABLE OF CONTENTS

Introduction... 6

Chapter 1: Getting Started 7

Found Objects 8
Beads 8
Tools and Supplies 11
Work Area 14
Beading Tips and Techniques 14

Chapter 2: The Weaving Stitches 17

Right-Angle Weave 18
Ladder Stitch 21
Basic Even-Number Flat Peyote Stitch (Gourd Stitch) 22
Vertical Netting or Lattice Weave 24
Backstitching 25
Couching 26

Chapter 3: Straps, Necklaces, and Fringe 27

The Straps 28
    Simple Stringing 28
    Scalloped Peyote 29
    Potawatomi Weave 30
    Spiral Rope 31
    Herringbone Chain (Chevron) 32
    Right-Angle Weave Variations 33
The Fringe 34
    Straight Fringe 34
    Branched Fringe 34
    Looped Fringe 35
    Twisted Fringe 35
Gallery 36

Chapter 4: Beading a Cabochon 37

Leopard Skin Agate Brooch 38
Bronze Septarian Necklace 42
Root Beer Septarian Necklace 44
Potawatomi Septarian Necklace 46
Marble Moon Man Necklace 48
Amethyst Crystal Necklace 51
Imperial Jasper Necklace and Earrings 54
Fluorite Slab Necklace 57
Magnifying Glass Necklace 60
Painted Stone Doughnut Necklace 62
Gallery 64

Chapter 5: Wearable Hardware 65
Drawer-Pull Lariat 66
Heavy-Metal Necklace 68
Key-Plate Necklace 70
Copper Elbow Choker 72
Fuses Bracelet 74
Gallery 76

Chapter 6: All That Glitters Might Be Glass 77

Green Perfume Bottle Necklace 78
Chinese Pottery Necklace 82
Beach Glass Necklace 84
Beaded Bottle Earrings 86

Chapter 7: Something's Fishy 89

Spinners and Eye Pins Set 90
Fish Worm Necklace and Earrings 92
Swivels Jewelry Set 94
Gallery 96

Chapter 8: Playing Games with Beading 97

Dominoes Necklace and Earrings 98
Scrabble Tile Bracelet 100
Mahjongg Tile Necklace 102
Mahjongg Tile Brooch 104

Chapter 9: Buttons and Coins 107

Pearl-and-Gold Button Necklace 108
Old Button Necklace 110
Chinese Coin Necklace 112
Gallery 114

Chapter 10: Shells and Other Natural Things 115

Beaded Gourd Necklace 116
Shell Brooch 118
Crystal Point Necklace 120
Leather Pouch Necklace 122
Gallery 124

Resources 126

Contributors 127

About the Author 128

INTRODUCTION

Some things you really can blame your siblings for. Such is the case with my bead addiction. I can place the blame squarely on the shoulders of my sister. It was Gloria who wanted me to accompany her to the bead store, which seemed an innocent enough request at the time. Little did I know where that innocent trip would lead me. Thinking back on that time, I can't help but think about the lamb-going-to-slaughter analogy.

I stood there in that small shop that was actually about the size of my living room and a whole world of possibilities opened up before me. I wanted to buy everything I saw. Unfortunately, I had to settle on a few tubes of seed beads and some bugle beads. I took them home, but since I had no idea what I was going to do with them, I put them away.

Periodically, I would take them out and admire them. I was mesmerized by the glitter and loved the feel of them. I was badly smitten. Eventually a design began to unfold in my brain, and I set about making it up. That, of course, led to another design, and another, and then the need for more beads. You know how it goes. I had become a "beadaholic."

My quest for knowledge of beading led me to combining non-beads with my beaded creations. Back when I was a practicing silversmith, I set cabochon gemstones in silver rings and pendants. I wanted to do that again but with beads as the medium. I figured out how it was done and set about doing some pieces. I was truly hooked once again.

Using the cabochons led me to wondering just what other non-bead stuff was out there that I could incorporate into my pieces. While shopping with my husband at some of his favorite places, I started looking for items that could be used in jewelry. I shopped for such items at hardware stores, flea markets, and fishing tackle stores as well as my usual haunts. Some things I found just lying around the house. I decided you could make jewelry out of all sorts of things.

Now it is time to pass some of my knowledge on beading with found objects on to others. Each project made with a found object will require different skills to turn it into jewelry, so I have laid this book out with that in mind. There are instructions on the basic items you will need, stitches, straps, fringes, and bead setting stones. Since it is likely that you will not be able to "find" the same objects I have, it was my intent to give you the tools you need to set about doing your own thing. Also included in the book are examples of other "found object" jewelry by beaders from around the country to give you a wider feel for the subject of found object jewelry and what you can do with it. The projects contain a variety of ideas from simple to complex.

It is my hope that you find lots of inspiration in these pages to make some beautiful found object jewelry of your own.

Carole Rodgers

GETTING STARTED

Most crafts require some basic tools and materials, and beading is certainly no exception. This chapter will cover those basic materials. You will not use all of these on every project, but if you do a lot of beading, you will eventually use most of them. If finances are a concern, buy what you need when you need it and add to your tools and materials as you can. It won't take long to find you have more stuff than you have room to store.

FOUND OBJECTS

You can use just about anything as jewelry as long as it meets a few parameters. Size, weight, and fragility are important factors to consider. Avoid sharp edges. Most of the things to consider can be judged by using common sense. Something that might work for a necklace might not be suitable for a bracelet because the item would be more prone to getting knocked about. It's nice if your object has a hole in it, but a hole is not essential for making jewelry out of an item.

BEADS

The most basic material needed when making beaded jewelry is, of course, beads. Since most beads are imported and many come from small factories, it is a wise idea to buy more beads than you think you will need for any project. There is often a vast difference in dye lots even though a bead may have the same number or color description. The same colors also vary greatly from one manufacturer to the next. Often beads are manufactured for a very short time, and you will never find them again. Of course, those same beads may show up many years later being sold as vintage beads.

Seed Beads

Seed beads are very small like seeds—hence their name. The two kinds of seed beads I recommend for bead weaving are Czech and Japanese. They are more uniform in size than those from other countries. With a few exceptions, the seed beads used in this book are all Japanese. They have larger holes. In bead weaving, it's often necessary to pass through the bead multiple times.

There are a number of sizes of seed beads used in this book—6°, 8°, 11°, and 14°. Seed beads are sized by a number with an "°" symbol behind it or sometimes with a "/0" behind the number. That symbol stands for "ought" and comes from an old way of numbering beads. Just remember that the larger the number, the smaller the bead.

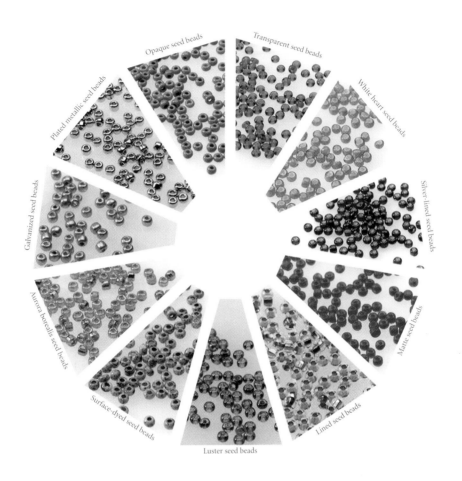

Opaque seed beads

Transparent seed beads

White heart seed beads

Plated metallic seed beads

Silver-lined seed beads

Galvanized seed beads

Aurora borealis seed beads

Matte seed beads

Surface-dyed seed beads

Lined seed beads

Luster seed beads

Bead Finishes

There is a wide range of finishes on beads, and more are being developed all the time. These finishes are used on beads other than seed beads. The following list is a brief reference to the most common bead finishes.

Opaque: Solid-colored beads, often seen in Native American beadwork.

Transparent: Clear or colored glass that is see-through.

White hearts: Colored glass around a white center, which is the heart.

Silver-lined: Transparent beads with a silver lining in the holes. They are quite bright and shiny, but the disadvantage is that the silver may tarnish or wear off over time.

Matte: The dull finish on these beads is made by etching or tumbling.

Lined: Instead of a silver lining, these beads have a color that is usually different from the glass color painted inside the holes.

Luster/lustre: Beads with a transparent, colored coating on them. The finish is often called Ceylon. Pearl beads are made this way.

Surface-dyed: Process used on all sorts of beads to make the difficult colors like purple and pink. The color can wear off or fade over time. Do not use these beads on any project that will be worn or handled a lot.

Aurora borealis (AB) or iridescent: These beads have a permanent rainbow-colored finish.

Galvanized metallic: The metallic coating on these beads is very thin and will wear off in time. Do not use these beads in anything that will be handled or worn.

Plated metallic: Beads with a metal plating on them. They retain their color well and are expensive.

Larger Beads

There are a lot of different beads used in this book. They are made from a wide variety of materials. Use high-quality glass beads but also try gemstone beads, as well as beads made from shells, wood, plastic, bone, rubber, or even natural seeds.

Bone: A popular bead material that can be carved, ground, painted, or dyed.

Bugle beads: Long, thin beads from 2mm to 30mm long in a variety of finishes. They can be straight, twisted, or hex-cut.

Faceted: Any bead that is ground with one or more flat surfaces.

Gemstone and semiprecious: Semiprecious gemstones carved or ground into beads. They come in a large variety of sizes and shapes.

Lampworked or artisan: Handmade beads made one at a time by wrapping molten glass around a mandrel in an open flame.

Metal: Beads made out of any number of different metals. Many used in jewelry are made from precious metals or are base metal plated with precious metals.

Plastic: A material readily used in bead production, alhough not popular for high-end jewelry. It can imitate any number of materials like gemstones and glass.

Polymer clay: Beads from polymer clay are getting more available in bead shops. They are usually made from canes like millefiori glass and have interesting patterns.

Pressed glass: Beads molded when the glass is still soft. They can be made in almost any size or shape.

Shell: Beads shaped from the shell material or small shells actually drilled so the entire shell becomes a bead.

Swarovski crystals: Made in Austria, these beads have a high lead content and are precision-faceted.

Wood: Beads made from any number of different kinds of wood, often carved, painted, or dyed.

SUPPLIES AND TOOLS

The following supplies and tools are useful to have available when you are ready to make that gorgeous creation. As with beads, when it comes to buying findings, threads, and needles, try to have more available than you think you will need because you will find yourself changing things.

Findings

Findings is the term generally used for all the hardware needed to finish a piece of jewelry. Findings come in base and precious metals. You will need some of the following basic findings before you start.

Bead tip: Used at the ends of bead strands mostly to hide the knot. (I prefer bottom-hole clamshell tips that close around your knot to hide it from view.)

Clasp: A closure used to join the ends of the piece of jewelry together.

Crimp bead: Small, soft metal bead in silver or gold color and of varying size that is crimped around the bead wire to hold the strand to a clasp or other part of the jewelry.

Earring findings: Come in a variety of configurations like wires, ball and post, and clips. Hoops are available to attach to the findings as well.

Eye pin: Pin that has an eye already turned on one end and often used to link two things together. Beads can be threaded on, and the pin is then cut and a loop is made in the other end.

Head pin: Long, straight pin with a flat head on one end like a straight pin without a point. Beads can be threaded on them, the pin is then cut to the correct length, and a loop is turned in the end so they can be hung.

Jump ring: Small ring of wire, sized in millimeters, used to join parts of a piece of jewelry together.

Pin back: Attached to the back of a piece to make a brooch. They come in different lengths.

Split ring: Double jump ring that looks like a very tight spring and will not split apart if it has tension on it.

Strand spacer: Bar with a number of holes in it used to hold the strands apart when a piece is worn.

Clasps

Jump rings

Split rings

Bead tips

Pin backs

Earring findings

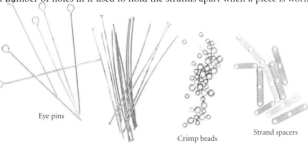

Eye pins

Head pins

Crimp beads

Strand spacers

Needles

You can use any needle to bead with that will go through your bead. However, a heavier needle is nice when you are stringing larger beads with larger holes, and if you are going to do bead weaving or use smaller beads, you will definitely want to buy beading needles.

Beading: Thinner and longer than regular sewing needles, ranging from size 10 to size 22, with 22 being the thinnest. The size numbers loosely refer to the size of beads that they will pass through. They also come in different lengths. Because bead needles are so thin, they bend easily. Keep a number on hand.

Sharps: Short, sharp pointed needles used for bead embroidery that are also useful for doing cabochon beading on leather.

Tapestry: Blunt pointed needles used for counted embroidery that are also useful for stringing bigger beads.

Wire beading: Fine, twisted wire needles with a loop where the eye should be that are used for thicker threads like silk knotting cord.

Threads and Stringing Materials

Different threads have different strengths and that is an important factor in choosing the kind of thread you use for beading. You want the strongest thread you can use to get the effect you desire.

Braided filament: Made up of multiple filaments braided together into an exceptionally strong thread, comes in several diameters, has almost no stretch, resists abrasion, and is difficult to cut with regular scissors (use blade scissors instead). It is also 100 percent water-resistant and will not rot in water like other threads. It does not come in a lot of colors, but can be colored with permanent marking pens.

Kevlar: Incredibly strong thread that is used in making bulletproof vests. It is naturally yellow and can be dyed darker with regular fabric dyes.

Memory wire: A rigid, pre-coiled steel wire that remembers its coiled shape. It comes in necklace, bracelet, and ring sizes.

Nymo: Probably the most common thread used for beading. It is made of non-twisted bonded nylon filaments, resists mildew, and doesn't rot. It comes in a variety

of thicknesses and colors and comes in sizes designated by letters OO, O, B, and D, with OO being the thinnest and D the thickest. It does stretch a little, so it is wise to give your piece of thread a gentle pull to remove part of the stretch before starting to bead with it.

Silamide: A twisted nylon tailoring thread with a waxy feel that is widely used for bead weaving. It comes in a variety of colors. In thickness, it is similar to Nymo O.

Stringing wire: Usually made up of a number of strands of extremely fine wire that are twisted together and then coated with a plastic film to prevent tarnishing. These wires work well for stringing bigger beads and ones that have sharp edges that might cut nylon or silk threads.

Thread conditioner: A beeswax product used on thread to keep it from tangling.

Tools

There are a number of tools that all beaders should have. Buy the best quality tools you can afford and learn to use them correctly. Good tools are usually easier to use, break less often, and provide better results.

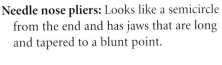

Bead gauge: A sliding ruler that allows you to accurately measure the size of beads in inches and millimeters. It is not essential, but can be quite helpful.

Bead sorting dish: A ceramic, plastic, or metal dish or set of triangle dishes to pour beads into to keep them separate as you work. Some beaders use a piece of felt, suede, Ultrasuede™, or Velux™ to lay beads on. The rough surface of these materials keeps the beads from moving around.

Chain nose pliers: Has wider, smooth jaws that do not taper down to sharp points. Used for bending wire at right-angles.

Crimp pliers: Designed specifically for doing a professional job of attaching crimp beads. It works in a two-step process whereby the bead is first crimped around the wire and then folded over back onto itself.

Needle nose pliers: Looks like a semicircle from the end and has jaws that are long and tapered to a blunt point.

Round nose pliers: Has smooth, round jaws that taper to fine points. Used for making wire loops, like in the ends of head and eye pins.

Scissors: Used for cutting thread.

Split ring pliers: Designed to be used with split rings, they separate the rings to make it easier to attach to your item.

Tool or storage box: A container to keep your work in. Although a personal decision, the fishing tackle section of many stores provides a wide variety of portable storage solutions.

Wire cutter: Looks like a pair of pliers but is specifically used for cutting wire. Use one of these when using stringing wire.

Glue

The three main glues used on these projects are shown in the photo and are my favorites. They are, however, just three glues of many that are available.

Fabri-Tac™: Used to attach leather to leather.

Gem-Tac™: Used for attaching stones and metal pieces to leather and other surfaces.

Pasco® Fix Industrial Adhesive: Used to adhere metal balls on the end of memory wire and metal parts together.

WORK AREA

Where a bead artist chooses to work is a personal preference. I work in my favorite rocking chair in the living room with a pillow-bottomed lap tray for a work surface. I have a light directly overhead and a magnifying lamp on the table beside me. Others choose to work at a table or counter and still others have a studio.

No matter where you choose to work, there are a few things you do need to be comfortable. First, find a comfortable chair. Back support is essential, as bending over while beading can be very stressful to your back muscles—not to mention your bottom muscles. Secondly, ensure good light. No matter your age, a magnifying glass can be extremely useful at times. Finally, a comfortable work surface rounds out the list.

BEADING TIPS AND TECHNIQUES

My beading education mostly came from books. When I started beading, there were few classes being given where I live. A number of things were not covered in books—like finishing ends nicely and good knots to use. The following are tips I have learned elsewhere or made up on my own. You may find them useful.

Threading Your Needle

If you have a problem threading your needle, dampen the end of the thread and smooth it between your thumb and index fingernails. It will spread out slightly and get a little thinner so it can pass through the eye easier. The closer you hold the thread to its end, the easier it is to insert into the needle.

Where there are references to "single-thread your needle," you will just use one strand of thread. "Double-threading" means to pull the thread through the needle until the thread ends meet, and the needle is centered.

Changing Threads

In bead weaving, sooner or later you will run out of thread in the middle of your work. My favorite way to add a new thread is to use a weaver's knot. If you get proficient at using this knot, you can change threads in the middle of a project without it being noticeable. The instructions are detailed on the facing page.

Weaver's Knot

A weaver's knot is a very effective way to join two threads together in the middle of a project.

1 Referring to Figure 1-1, A is the end of the old thread and B is the end of the new thread. Cross them and hold between thumb and forefinger at point C. D is the new thread.

2 Pass D around and over A, up under B, and over A again, as shown in Figure 1-2.

3 Then turn A down over D, over the new thread B, and through the loop made by D, as shown in Figure 1-3.

4 Bring end B down and hold it with end A. Pull D tight, making sure you have pulled A down to where you want the knot. This knot slips through most seed beads and holds very well without being glued.

5 When you have tied on the new thread, weave the old end back through the work, being sure to tie an overhand knot after a few beads.

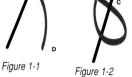

Figure 1-1

Figure 1-2

Figure 1-3

Overhand Knot

Overhand knots are used most often to weave in thread ends.

1 Take a small stitch over a thread between two beads in your work and pull the thread through until you have just a small loop of thread left.

2 Pass the needle through the loop, as shown in Figure 1-4, and pull tight.

3 Pass through a few beads and tie another overhand knot.

4 Apply a very small amount of glue to the thread close to the knot and pass through a few more beads.

5 Pull the thread tightly and cut off the excess thread close to a bead.

Figure 1-4

Square Knot

A square knot is a good knot for ending threads and can also be used to change threads in the middle of a piece.

1 Cross the thread in your right hand over the thread in your left hand, around, and through to tie the knot, as shown in Figure 1-5.

Figure 1-5

2 Take the thread that's now in your left hand over the thread in your right hand, around, and through to tie another knot, as shown in Figure 1-6.

3 Put a small amount of glue on the knot to make sure it stays secure.

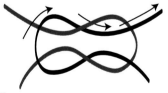

Figure 1-6

Breaking a Bead

Occasionally, you will get a bead in the wrong spot. If it is a seed bead, it's usually easier to break the bead than to tear out your work. You want to be very careful when breaking a bead, though. If you use pliers and attempt to smash it, you will break the thread. To avoid thread breaks, try the following method.

1 Tighten the thread over your finger so the bead pops up away from the thread.

2 Grab the bead with the middle of your pliers, perpendicular to the hole and above the thread.

3 Turn your face away and squeeze the pliers until the bead breaks.

Tip

I usually break beads over a wastebasket or under a towel to avoid flying glass. If you must look, be sure to wear protective eye gear. Glass in the eye is not fun!

Using a Stop Bead

A stop bead is tied on close to the end of your thread to keep beads from slipping off the thread. Simply tie it on with a half-knot so that it can easily be undone later. You will later remove the bead and use the thread to finish your project.

Ending a Strand

I have tried a number of ways to end my beaded strands so they will look professional. I find that the following methods work best for me.

Option 1

1. If you use bead wire for your strand, end that strand by threading on a crimp bead, then passing through your clasp or jump/split ring, and back through the crimp bead into your bead strand. Be sure to pull the wire snug.

2. Using your crimp pliers, bend the crimp bead tightly around the wire to secure.

3. Work wire through the beading for about ½" and trim the end so it is hidden in the beads.

Option 2

1. Make the closure an integral part of your beaded piece by beading a loop at the end of one strand.

2. Attach a button or large bead on the other end to hook the loop over.

Option 3

For longer necklaces—ones that will slip easily over the head—I often skip the clasp entirely. A strand without a clasp is actually more comfortable to wear, especially on a bare neck.

Option 4 (My Favorite)

1. Pass the thread through the crimp bead and tie several square knots around the crimp bead.

2. Take the thread through the bottom hole of the clamshell bead tip, as shown in Figure 1-7 to begin necklace.

3. Glue the knots, trim the threads, and close the clamshell around the crimp bead, as shown in Figure 1-8.

4. Bend the bar of the clamshell tip around in a loop (Figure 1-9).

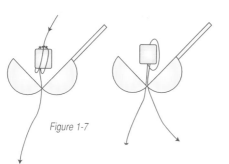

Figure 1-7

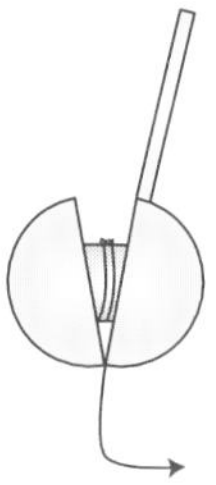

Figure 1-8

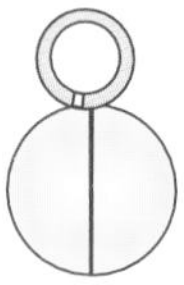

Figure 1-9

Option 5

1. When using heavier thread/bead wire, thread on a crimp bead before threading on the clamshell bead tip.

2. String on a second crimp bead.

3. Pass the thread/wire back through the clamshell tip hole, the first crimp bead, and then back through the beading.

4. Secure the crimp bead on the strand.

5. Trim the thread/wire ends.

6. Close the clamshell around the second crimp bead. This gives you a nicer looking end to your thread.

THE WEAVING STITCHES

Chapter 2

The subject of weaving stitches in beading is a vast one. There is no way to cover all of them here. Instead, I will concentrate on those that have been used in the projects done for this book. A basic knowledge of these stitches is all you need to know to do most of the projects and to give a platform for doing your own thing.

RIGHT-ANGLE WEAVE

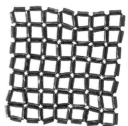

There are two ways to do right-angle weave—with one needle or with two. Either one results in the same look. Try both methods and choose the one you prefer.

Right-angle weave is composed of patterns of four beads. These patterns are called squares. If you use bugle beads or other straight beads, the pattern does make a square. If you use round beads, however, the pattern will look more like a diamond.

Right-angle weave does not work well with all beads. Bugles, rounds, ovals, and bicones generally work the best. If you are unsure, try your beads to see if they will work.

Both of these samples were done in right-angle weave. Note how the beads make a difference in how the pattern looks.

Double-Needle Right-Angle Weave

1 Place a needle on each end of your thread, being sure to keep the thread in the needles even in length.

2 String four beads on one needle and center them on the thread.

3 Pass the second needle through the last bead you picked up from the opposite direction and pull up snug to form a square or diamond shape centered on your thread, as shown in Figure 2-1. You can use more than one bead per side, but the pattern in regular right-angle weave will always have four sides.

Figure 2-1

4 To continue, string two beads on one needle and one on the second needle and then pass the second needle through the last bead on the first needle and pull up snugly, creating two squares as in Figure 2-2.

5 Continue in this manner until you are one square short of your desired length. You are continuously doing a figure-eight pattern with the two needles.

Figure 2-2

6 For the last square of the first row, thread three beads on one needle and pass the second needle back through the last bead from the opposite direction so that the threads are coming out of the side of the pattern, as shown in Figure 2-3.

Figure 2-3

7 To turn the corner to start the second row, thread three beads on the thread closest to the end of the piece, pass the second needle through the last bead from the opposite direction, and pull snugly to create a square on one side of the first row, as shown in Figure 2-4.

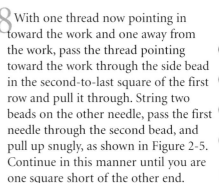

Figure 2-4

8 With one thread now pointing in toward the work and one away from the work, pass the thread pointing toward the work through the side bead in the second-to-last square of the first row and pull it through. String two beads on the other needle, pass the first needle through the second bead, and pull up snugly, as shown in Figure 2-5. Continue in this manner until you are one square short of the other end.

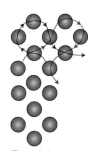
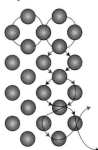

Figure 2-5

9 To finish the second row, pass the thread through the side bead of the first row and string two beads on that needle. Pass the second needle through the last bead and pull up snugly, again referring to Figure 2-5.

10 With one thread pointing away from the work and the other pointing down the work, string three beads on the thread that points away, pass the second needle through the last bead from the opposite direction, and pull up snugly. You are ready for the third row. Continue going up and down adding rows until your piece is the width you want.

Double-Needle Right-Angle Weave (*continued*)

Joining the ends:

If you want to make a tube of your right-angle piece, you will need to lace the piece together at its ends.

1 Bring the ends around so they meet as in Figure 2-6.

Figure 2-6

2 Cut a length of thread and place a needle on each end.

3 Thread on one bead and pass each needle through the side bead of the bottom pattern on each end. String one bead on one needle, pass the second needle through it from the opposite direction, and pull snugly. Pass each needle through the next two side beads and repeat adding a bead, as in Figure 2-7.

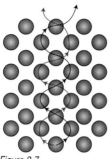

Figure 2-7

When joining the ends, you are adding another row of patterns to the piece. So if you want 21 rows of squares, you should weave 20 rows before joining. The joining row then becomes the final row.

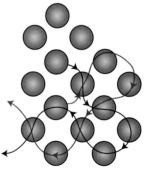

The Green Perfume Bottle Necklace, shown here and with detailed instructions on page 78, contains right-angle weave.

Adding a shorter row:

1 If you would like to decrease your piece by one square, work out to the end of a row, bringing your threads out the end bead.

2 Weave the threads back through the last square.

3 When you come to the next square, weave back through it like you are turning the corner. You are then ready to begin the first square of the shorter row. See Figure 2-8. If you want to decrease by more than one square, you will have to work back through more squares before you start your decrease.

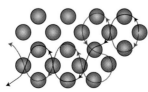

Figure 2-8

Adding a longer row:

1 To increase the length of a row, weave your threads so they come out the end bead.

2 String on three beads and turn the corner as usual, as in Figure 2-9. If you want to increase by more than one square, do the number of squares you need and turn the corner as usual.

Figure 2-9

Single-Needle Right-Angle Weave

1 Cut a length of thread and single-thread your needle. String on four beads and tie them together in a square knot between beads one and four, close to the end of your thread, as shown in Figure 2-10. Be careful not to tie them too tightly as you need a little wiggle room.

Figure 2-10

2 Pass your needle and thread back through beads 1, 2, and 3, as in Figure 2-11.

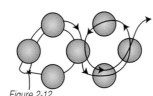

Figure 2-11

3 String on three more beads (5, 6, and 7). Pass back through bead 3 of the first square and then through beads 5 and 6 in the second square, as in Figure 2-12.

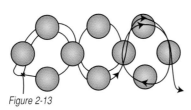

Figure 2-12

4 String on three more beads (8, 9, and 10) and pass back through beads 6, 8, and 9, as shown in Figure 2-13. Continue picking up three beads for each new square until you have the desired length.

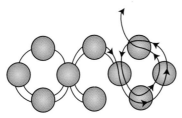

Figure 2-13

5 To turn the corner to begin the second row, pass the needle back through the last three beads of the last square of the row and bring the needle out the top bead as in Figure 2-14.

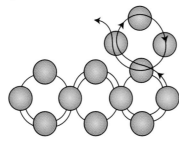

Figure 2-14

6 String on three beads and pass the needle back through the top bead, forming the first square of the second row as in Figure 2-15.

Figure 2-15

7 From this point on, string on two new beads for each square, passing the needle through the next top bead of the previous row and the last bead of the previous square, as shown in Figure 2-16.

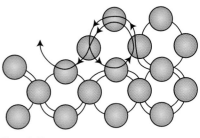

Figure 2-16

Adding a longer row:

1 To increase the length of your pattern, make an extra square on the end of your row as shown in Figure 2-17.

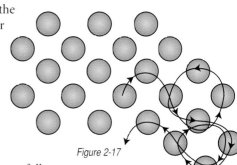

Figure 2-17

2 Turn the corner, follow the thread path, and proceed down your extended row as shown in the illustration. If you wish to increase by more than one square, then do that number of squares on the end of the row and proceed in the same manner.

Adding a shorter row:

1 To decrease a row by one square, follow the thread path in Figure 2-18 back through your work to the second-to-last square.

2 Come out the bottom bead to turn the corner and start your next row. If you want to decrease by more than one square, work your thread back through the number of squares you wish to decrease by and continue as in Figure 2-18. Do not cross open areas between beads.

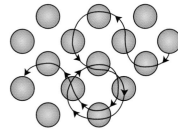

Figure 2-18

LADDER STITCH

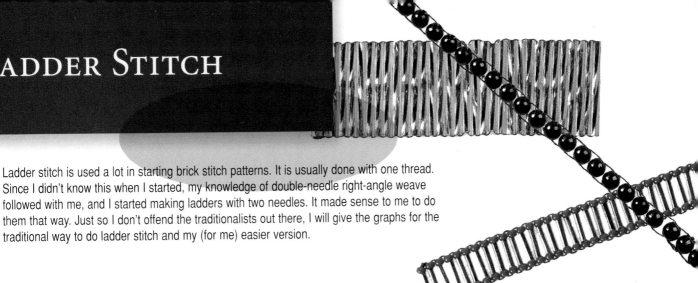

Ladder stitch is used a lot in starting brick stitch patterns. It is usually done with one thread. Since I didn't know this when I started, my knowledge of double-needle right-angle weave followed with me, and I started making ladders with two needles. It made sense to me to do them that way. Just so I don't offend the traditionalists out there, I will give the graphs for the traditional way to do ladder stitch and my (for me) easier version.

Single-Needle Ladder Stitch

1 Single-thread your needle and string on two beads. Tie the thread in a knot so that the beads sit side by side.

2 Referring to Figure 2-19, pass the needle through the second bead, string on a third bead, pass the needle back through the second bead, and then the third.

3 String on a fourth bead, pass back through the third, and then the fourth. Continue in this manner until you reach your desired length.

Figure 2-19

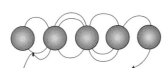

A finished ladder should look like Figure 2-20 (above), except that the beads should be tight side-by-side.

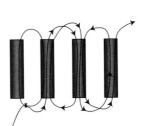

Figure 2-21 shows the same ladder, only this time with bugle beads.

Figure 2-22 shows how a combination of bugle and seed beads should look when the thread has passed through.

Double-Needle Ladder Stitch

1 Place a needle on each end of your thread and string two beads on one needle and pass the second needle through the last bead from the opposite direction.

2 String a third bead on one needle and pass the second needle through it from the opposite direction, as in Figure 2-23. Note: The thread is shown in two colors in the illustration so you can see how the thread passes back and forth through the beads.

3 Continue in this manner until you reach the desired length.

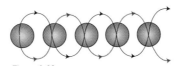

Figure 2-23

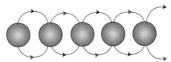

Figure 2-24 (above) shows how the ladder should look after the thread passes through, except that the beads should be tight side-by-side.

Figure 2-25 (above) is the same thing done with bugle beads.

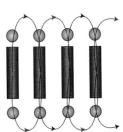

Figure 2-26 is done with seed and bugle beads. The pattern works the same no matter how many beads you have in your ladder. Just remember to pull the beads up snugly so they sit side-by-side.

BASIC EVEN-NUMBER FLAT PEYOTE STITCH (GOURD STITCH)

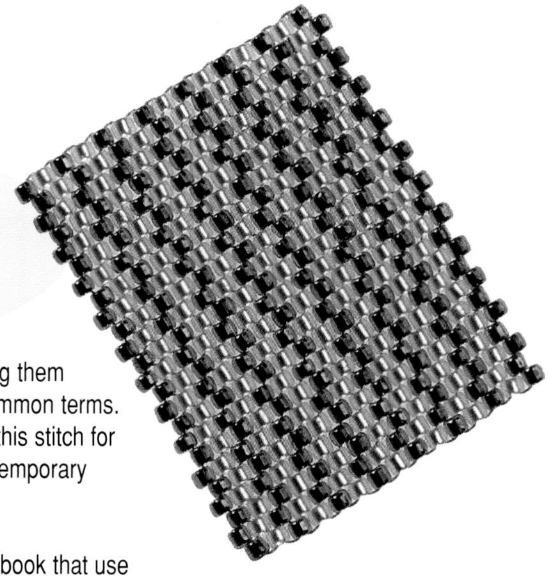

This stitch has been around for hundreds of years and has several names, among them diagonal, twill, gourd and Peyote stitch. Gourd stitch and Peyote are the most common terms. The term "Peyote" is used by Native Americans to describe beadwork done with this stitch for religious and ceremonial purposes. "Peyote" seems to be the most common contemporary name for this stitch.

There are a number of variations in Peyote stitch, but most of the projects in this book that use Peyote are done with the basic stitch. It is an extremely useful stitch in bead-setting cabochons.

The beads in Peyote stitch are offset like paving bricks. They are stacked on each other in columns vertically as you make the rows horizontally. Because the beads are offset by half of a bead, it is easier to count the rows on a diagonal.

Basic Even-Number Flat Peyote

1 Using one size of beads, single-thread your needle and tie a stop bead within 4" of the end of your thread.

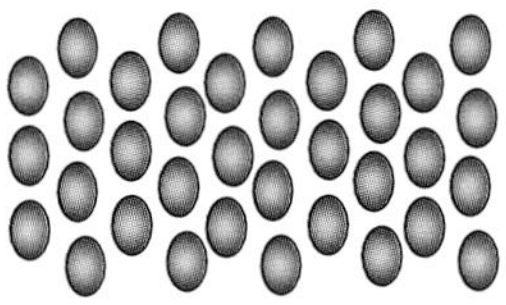

Here is how the Peyote pattern works up.

2 Thread on 11 beads, as shown in Figure 2-27. These beads will count as the first two rows of your piece.

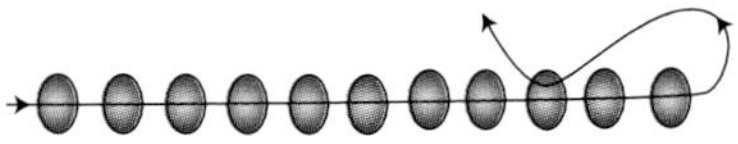

3 Referring again to Figure 2-27, pass your thread through the third bead from the needle end. Hold the third bead as you pass through it.

Figure 2-27

4 Pull the thread all the way through so that the first bead is resting on the second bead as in Figure 2-28. You may have to move it into position.

Figure 2-28

5 Pick up another bead with your needle and pass through the fifth bead, as in Figure 2-29.

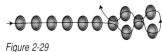
Figure 2-29

6 Continue in this manner until you get to the end of the row, as in Figure 2-30. Push each set of two beads together to tighten the work. You may remove the stop bead at this time and tie the two threads in a knot or leave it and work the tail in later. Note: Your piece now has an up-and-down appearance. The beads that stick up are called "up-beads."

Figure 2-30

7 String on a new bead and pass through the second bead from the end (an up-bead), as shown in Figure 2-31.

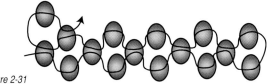
Figure 2-31

8 String on another bead and pass through the next up-bead. Continue like this to the end of the row and continue adding beads and rows in this manner until you have your desired size.

Basic Even-Number Flat Peyote *(continued)*

Increasing the beadwork:

If you are covering an odd-shaped article with Peyote stitch, you may find the need to increase or decrease your beading at some point in the piece. Such methods of increasing and decreasing are useful when needed to cover an article like the Beaded Gourd Necklace, page 116. There are ways to increase and decrease on the edges of a piece as well; however, we will not cover those here since none of the projects contained within require edge increases/decreases.

1 To make a simple increase in the middle of a row, use two beads instead of one at the point in which you want the increase, as shown in Figure 2-32. Try to use beads that are more narrow than most.

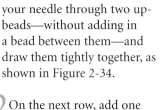
Figure 2-32

2 When you make the next row, add one bead between the two narrow beads, as in Figure 2-33.

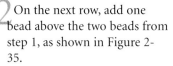
Figure 2-33

3 Continue weaving as before the increase.

Decreasing the beadwork:

1 To make a simple decrease in the middle of a row, run your needle through two up-beads—without adding in a bead between them—and draw them tightly together, as shown in Figure 2-34.

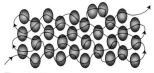
Figure 2-34

2 On the next row, add one bead above the two beads from step 1, as shown in Figure 2-35.

Figure 2-35

3 Continue working as usual on the next row, as in Figure 2-36. You have decreased your work by the width of two beads.

Figure 2-36

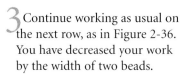

Figure 2-37   *Figure 2-38*

Figures 2-37 and 2-38 show how a straight pattern looks first by itself and then with a design through it.

Peyote stitch is used to cover the stem portion of a jewelry gourd in the Beaded Gourd Necklace, which is found on page 116.

Tip

If you are doing a pattern in Peyote stitch, you need to keep some things in mind. The beads that you string on at the very beginning become rows 1 and 2. When you go back along the row adding new beads, you are creating the third row. It is the third row beads that push or pull the first two rows of beads into place. Figure 2-37 shows how the pattern works up. As you progress in your pattern, keep close count of the rows since the count is very important in following patterns. It may help to remember that each row is only a half-bead wide. Count your rows diagonally for a correct count.

VERTICAL NETTING OR LATTICE WEAVE

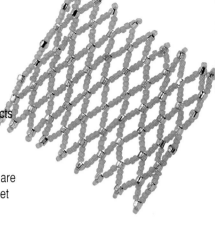

Vertical netting is a versatile and useful weave, particularly when using found objects. It covers objects nicely, especially round objects, because it can expand and contract very well to fit a shape.

Vertical netting makes a bead fabric that resembles a net with diamond-shaped holes. It is built by going up and down the piece vertically. The diamond hole sizes vary according to how many beads are in each section. Always use an odd number of sections because the diamonds fit together in an offset pattern. The pattern will not work with an even number of sections.

Basic Vertical Netting

1 Single-thread your needle and tie one "A" bead on the end in a single overhand knot so you can remove it easily later. Then string on one "B" bead, two "A" beads, one "B," repeating the pattern until you have five sections of the two "A" beads. End with one "B" and one "A." The completed pattern, as shown in Figure 2-39, should be: A-B-A-A-B-A-A-B-A-A-B-A-A-B-A-A-B-A.

2 Skip the last "A" bead you threaded on and pass back through the last "B" bead. (Be sure the beads in the first row are snug together at this point.)

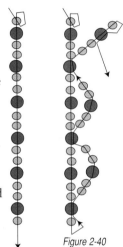

Figure 2-39

Figure 2-40

3 Referring to Figure 2-40, string on two "A" beads, one "B" bead, and two "A" beads and pass your needle through the third "B" bead from the bottom. Repeat A-A-B-A-A pattern again, pass through the fifth "B" bead from the bottom, and end the row with A-A-B-A pattern.

4 For each additional row, repeat steps 2 and 3, as in Figure 2-41.

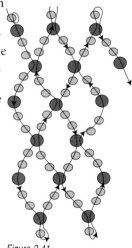

Figure 2-41

Vertical Netting Tube

1 To join the ends together to form a tube, bring the ends around to meet. Come out of the left bottom point "A" bead and pass through the "B" bead.

2 String on two "A" beads and immediately swing over to the next "B" bead on the right and pass through it.

3 String on two more "A" beads and pass through the "B" bead on the left.

4 Keep going back and forth across and up the piece, as shown in Figure 2-42, lacing it together until you get to the original "A" bead you tied on the end of your thread in the beginning.

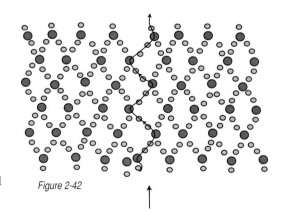

Figure 2-42

5 Either untie the half-knot and work the two threads through the piece to the end, or leave the knot around the bead and tie the two thread ends together and then work them back through the piece and tie them off. You can then run a thread through all the point beads to gather it to fit whatever object you want.

24

BACKSTITCHING

Backstitching is an embroidery stitch that is necessary to start a lot of projects—especially those that include something you want to bead around, like a cabochon. You can also use this stitch to embellish items like clothing.

In the chapter on beading around cabochons (Chapter 4, page 37), you will see that the first thing you need to do is glue the cabochon to a piece of backing material and allow it to dry. Then, make a line of beads around the cabochon with backstitching, so you can weave the beaded bezel.

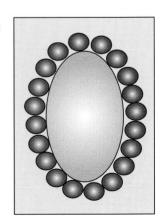

The Leopard Skin Agate Brooch (shown here) is the first project in Chapter 4 and utilizes backstitching to begin the beaded bezel.

1 Single-thread your needle with the strongest thread that will still pass through your beads about four times. At the end of the thread, tie a knot big enough so it won't pass through your backing material.

2 Bring the threaded needle up from the underside of the backing material in the middle of one side of the cabochon (or other item you are beading around) and about a half-bead width from the cabochon. Pull the thread through until the knot is tight against the backing material.

3 String on two beads, lay them tightly against the cabochon, and pass the needle back through the backing tight against the last bead. Then come up in the first hole again and pass through the beads one more time, as shown in Figure 2-43.

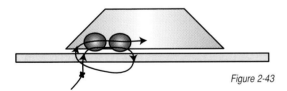

Figure 2-43

4 String on two more beads and take the needle down through the backing, tight against the new beads. Bring the needle up through the second hole and pass through the second set of beads again, as shown in Figure 2-44.

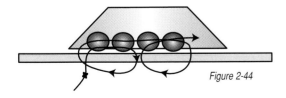

Figure 2-44

5 Thread on two new beads, as in Figure 2-45. Pass back through the backing, come up through the backing between the second two sets of beads, and pass through the new set.

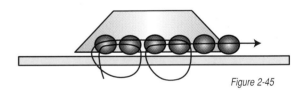

Figure 2-45

6 Repeat step 5 until you have completely encircled the cabochon (or other object) as in Figure 2-46.

7 To finish, pass the thread back through all the beads to tighten the ring. Then, pass thread to the underside and secure it in the stitching.

Figure 2-46

COUCHING

Couching is used to attach strings of beads to a backing material. The stitch does not actually go through the beads, but rather, over the thread that goes through the beads. Couching in this book is used mostly in beading around cabochons, as in Chapter 4, page 37. Couched beads are added after the initial beaded bezel is completed.

1 Thread your needle as you wish. Depending on the size of your beads, you may want to use a double-thread. At the end of the thread, tie a knot big enough so it won't pass through your backing material.

2 Pass the needle through the backing material from the underside and come up a half-bead width from where you want your beads to go. Begin stringing on enough beads to make a ring around your cabochon, as in Figure 2-47.

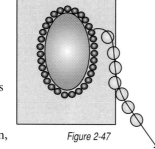

Figure 2-47

3 Snug up the string of beads around your beaded bezel, as in Figure 2-48, keeping in mind that the string will tighten up as you couch it in place.

4 When you have completed your ring of beads, pass back through the ring again to strengthen it. Take your needle and thread through to the underside of the backing material and tie off your thread by making a couple of passes through the stitches on the back, but do not cut it.

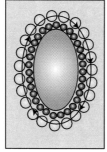

Figure 2-48

5 Bring your needle up in the middle of one side on the outside of your bead ring and very close to the beads, as shown in Figure 2-49.

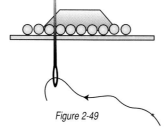

Figure 2-49

6 Take the needle up and over the bead ring and down directly opposite where you just came up through the backing, as in Figure 2-50. Pull your thread snug.

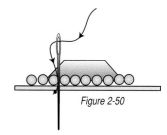

Figure 2-50

7 Go directly across the bead ring and make a stitch. Divide the two halves you have made and do a stitch in the center of each half. You will have a lot of thread crossing on the back, but no one will see it once you are done. It is advisable to do this to keep the bead ring evenly spaced. If you start at one point and proceed around the ring, you can get a pucker or a pull at the other end.

8 Start couching, as shown in Figure 2-51, between each bead if they are large beads, or every few if using seed beads. Bring your needle up at 1 and down directly across; up at 3 and down directly across; up at 5 and down directly across. Continue until you have gone completely around the ring.

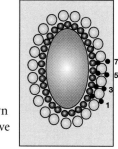

Figure 2-51

9 When you have completed couching around the piece, it would look like Figure 2-52—that is, if you could see it. The stitch pulls the bead string down into the backing material and out of sight. You can add as many rows of beads as you would like to your piece.

Figure 2-52

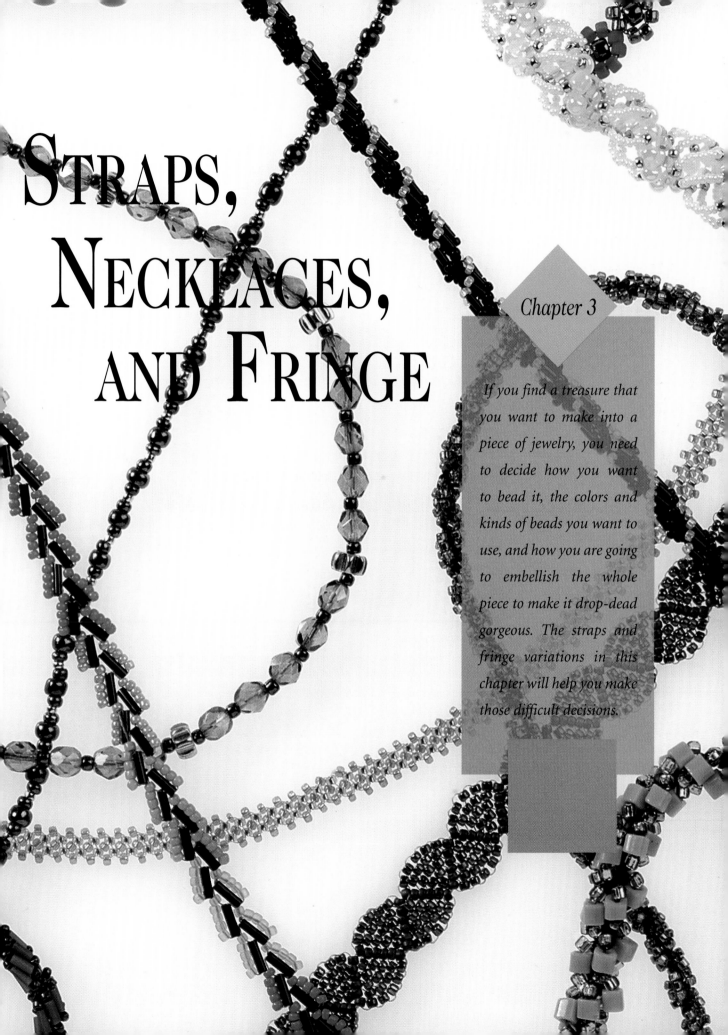

STRAPS, NECKLACES, AND FRINGE

Chapter 3

If you find a treasure that you want to make into a piece of jewelry, you need to decide how you want to bead it, the colors and kinds of beads you want to use, and how you are going to embellish the whole piece to make it drop-dead gorgeous. The straps and fringe variations in this chapter will help you make those difficult decisions.

Since most necklaces and neck straps are used to show off a "found" object, match the neck strap to the object for the best results. The necklace should enhance the overall appearance of the finished piece and should be an integral part of the whole. Try using a variety of beads to do each weave and see how the look changes drastically. Note the examples shown throughout this chapter of how using different beads can give you an entirely different look.

Simple Stringing

Simple stringing is making a necklace that is not bead-woven. It can be one or more strands, but the beads are simply threaded on a strand or strands and there is no passing back and forth through beads as in most bead weaving techniques.

When making a necklace in simple stringing, try to come up with a pleasing pattern for arranging the beads in your necklace. It is also usually a good idea to use different colors and shapes of beads, depending on what it is you wish to show off.

Sometimes, what defines your strand is the number of beads you have available to use. If you have just one type of bead to use, the problem is easily solved by doing a strand in all the same bead. Of course, that's boring and monotonous, so strive for two beads that go with each other. Then do a basic A-B-A-B pattern, or perhaps an A-B-B-A pattern, or B-A-A-B pattern. Keep in mind that even two bead strands can also be monotonous unless the beads are very different in size or shape.

Try to have at least three different beads to make up a pattern. This allows you to do a larger variety of patterns like A-B-C-B-A, or five patterns of A-B and then C, or any number of different configurations.

Having four or more beads to use, as in the two photos at right, makes for a more interesting strand. Often, you can use a simple bead pattern for the upper parts of your strand (closer to the neck) and intersperse the pattern with larger beads closer to your focal point.

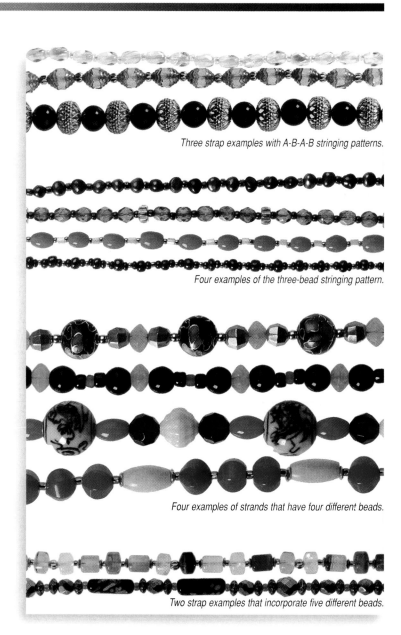

Three strap examples with A-B-A-B stringing patterns.

Four examples of the three-bead stringing pattern.

Four examples of strands that have four different beads.

Two strap examples that incorporate five different beads.

Scalloped Peyote

Berrie Butrick of Garretsville, Ohio, taught me this stitch at her booth at the Four Corners Swap Meet in Quartzsite, Arizona. I had never seen anything like the scalloped bands on some of her pieces. They resembled rickrack. Berrie's technique follows:

1 Weave a Peyote band six beads wide. Refer to Peyote instructions on pages 22 and 23. In this case, don't get concerned with good tension. Work very loosely because the looser your work, the more pronounced the scallop will be. The strap will shrink in size when it is completed. Leave your working thread in case you need to add additional beads to get the length you want. Your completed band should look very similar to Figure 3-1.

2 Double-thread a second needle with a new piece of thread longer than your strap and tie on a stop bead.

3 Starting at one end of the strap, pass your needle diagonally through the piece through six beads in a diagonal line to the other side of the band, pull the thread snugly, skip over to the next bead, and continue diagonally back across the band, moving back and forth across and down the piece in a zigzag pattern, as shown by the dark bead path in Figure 3-2. The strap will begin to gather and scallop.

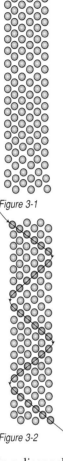

Figure 3-1

Figure 3-2

This beautiful necklace is one of Berrie Butrick's pieces with a scalloped Peyote band.

At left, from top: Notice how a Peyote strap normally looks, how you should work it for scalloped Peyote, how it zigzags when you pull it up, and how it looks when you use three sizes of beads.

Tip

Through experimentation, I found that if you use three different sizes of beads—14°, 11°, and 8°, for example—the piece will automatically curve in on itself when you pull up the zigzag, which results in a circular piece. This makes a lovely collar necklace.

Potawatomi Weave

Also in Quartzsite, Arizona, I met Donnie Cripe, who works at Hardies Beads. She was wearing a necklace made in Potawatomi weave and gave me some instructions on how to do it. It is a weave comprised of three beads on top of two beads.

1 Single-thread your needle and start with two colors of the same size bead (in this case, orange and blue).

2 String on two orange beads, one blue, one orange, and one blue bead. Take them to within 6" of the end of your thread and tie them into a circle with a double-knot, as shown in Figure 3-3. Be sure to keep your working thread to the left.

Figure 3-3

3 Hold the ring of beads with your left thumb and forefinger so your fingers just cover the two orange beads. (Use opposite hand if you are left-handed.) Thread on one blue, one orange, one blue, one orange, and one blue bead, as in Figure 3-4.

Figure 3-4

4 Pass your needle through the orange bead between the two blue ones in the first ring and through the first orange bead you picked up in the second pick-up, as shown in Figure 3-5. Note the direction the needle passes through the second orange bead. You are actually passing through the second orange bead in the opposite direction than you did on the first pass.

Figure 3-5

5 Pull the thread up snug until the three blue beads fall into a line above the two orange beads, as shown in Figure 3-6.

6 Work your thumb and forefinger up the piece as you complete each row and keep your thread tight. Then string on one blue, one orange, one blue, one orange, and one blue bead. Pass through the orange bead between the two blue ones in the second ring and through the first orange bead in the third pickup, as shown in Figure 3-6, and pull snug.

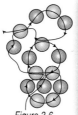

Figure 3-6

7 Continue working in this manner until you have the length you want, with the finished stitch looking like that illustrated in Figure 3-7.

Figure 3-7

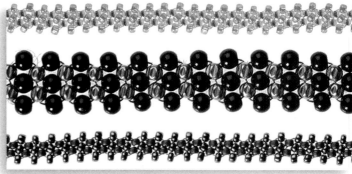

The Potawatomi Septarian Necklace, which is detailed on pages 46 and 47, shows just how spectacular this weave can look when used in jewelry-making.

As with the other stitches, the Potawatomi weave takes on different looks, depending on the size, color, type, and number of different beads used.

Spiral Rope

This stitch makes a lovely and very strong round rope because the thread passes through every core bead at least three times. Use beads with large holes, such as Japanese seed beads or slightly larger beads. This stitch can be done with a variety of bead sizes, each of which gives it a totally different look, as shown in the accompanying photo.

The instructions given here are for the basic stitch, using the same size beads. It is easier to learn if you use just two colors of beads. The illustrations show each bunch of three beads in a different color just so it is easier to differentiate each pass-through and how the beads fall into place as you weave.

1 Single-thread your needle and choose a color to be your core bead (the one that goes through the middle). It is not necessary to add a stop bead, as you will pass back through the beads in your first pass-through.

Figure 3-8

2 String on four of the core-beads and three of the outside beads, as shown in Figure 3-8.

Figure 3-9

3 Pass back through the four core beads, as in Figure 3-9, and pull the thread snugly. Push the core beads to the left. (Reverse this process if left-handed.)

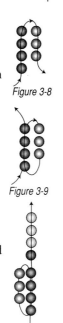

Figure 3-10

4 String on one core bead and three outside beads, as in Figure 3-10.

5 Skip the first core bead and pass the thread through the next three core beads from the bottom up. Then, pass through the core bead you just added, as in Figure 3-11. Push the outside beads to the left.

Figure 3-11

6 String on one core bead and three outside beads, as shown in Figure 3-12.

Figure 3-12

7 Skip the bottom two core beads and pass back through the next three beads and the core bead you just picked up, as in Figure 3-13. Pull snugly and push the outside beads to the left. Continue in this manner until the rope is as long as desired.

Figure 3-13

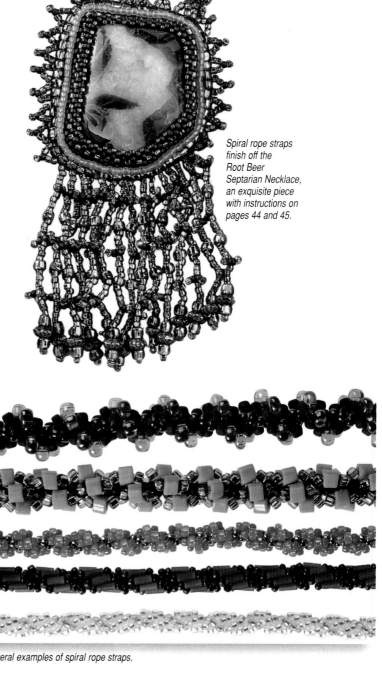

Spiral rope straps finish off the Root Beer Septarian Necklace, an exquisite piece with instructions on pages 44 and 45.

Several examples of spiral rope straps.

Herringbone (Chevron) Chain

This chain is called "herringbone," but I have also included the term "chevron" because I do not want to confuse it with Ndebele weave, which is also called herringbone but looks totally different. The herringbone chain uses seed and bugle beads set in pairs that are at angles to each other. You need to weave several patterns before it begins to fall into place nicely.

You will have to determine how many seed beads you need, depending on the size of the bugle bead used. The length of the seed beads should be slightly longer than the length of the bugle. The sample in the accompanying photo shows a #2 bugle with five 11° seed beads.

The Painted Stone Doughnut Necklace, shown here and with complete instructions on pages 62 and 63, features a herringbone chain with several bead colors.

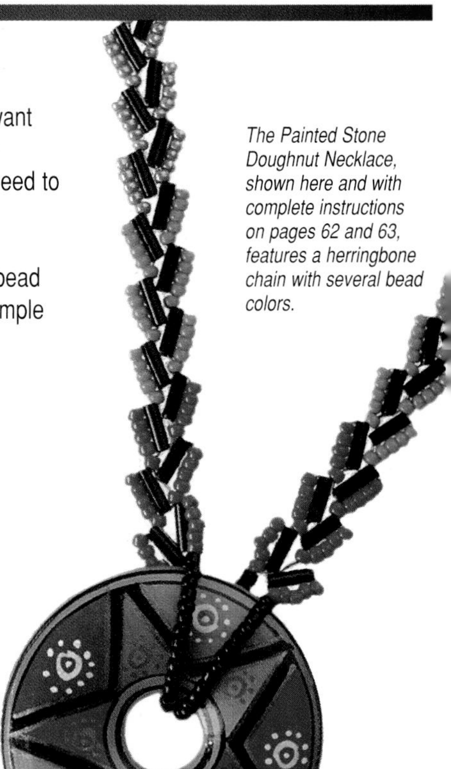

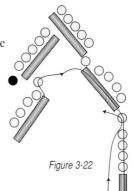

1 Tie a stop bead on the end of your thread, leaving a 6" tail. String on a bugle and five seed beads, as in Figure 3-14, and push them against the stop bead.

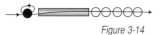

Figure 3-14

2 Pass through the bugle bead, as in Figure 3-15, and pull up snugly so the seed beads sit on the bugle.

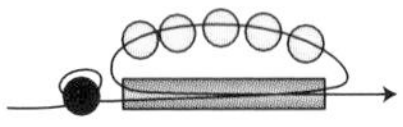

Figure 3-15

3 String on another bugle and five more seed beads, as in Figure 3-16, pushing them close to the first cluster.

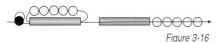

Figure 3-16

4 Pass the thread through the second bugle and pull up snugly, as shown in Figure 3-17.

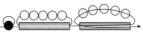

Figure 3-17

5 Fold the two clusters at an angle to each other, string on five seed beads and one bugle, and pass the thread up through the first seed bead you picked up, as shown in Figure 3-18. Note: The order you string on the beads changes with this step.

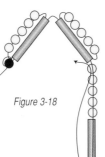

Figure 3-18

6 Pass the thread through the first bugle, as in Figure 3-19, and pull up snugly.

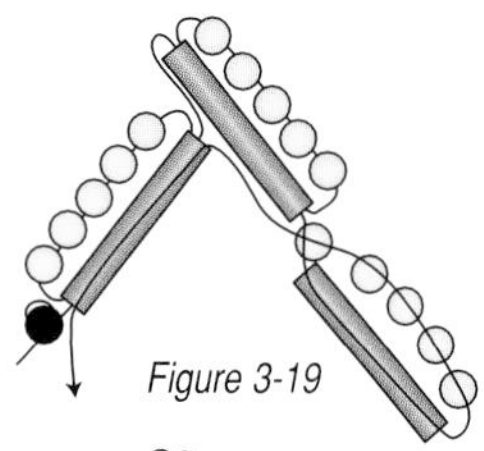

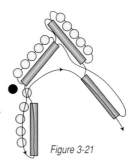

Figure 3-19

7 String on five seed beads and one bugle and pass the thread up through the first seed bead you added in this pass, as in Figure 3-20.

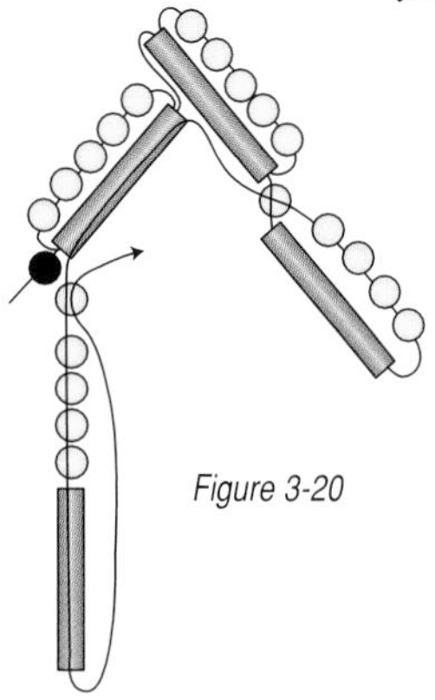

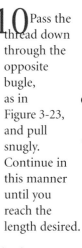

Figure 3-20

8 Pass the thread down the fourth bugle, as in Figure 3-21, and pull snugly to make the herringbone.

Figure 3-21

9 String on five seed beads and one bugle, pass the thread up through the first seed bead, as in Figure 3-22, and pull snugly.

Figure 3-22

10 Pass the thread down through the opposite bugle, as in Figure 3-23, and pull snugly. Continue in this manner until you reach the length desired.

Figure 3-23

11 When you reach the desired length, remove the stop bead and attach the clasp. Refer to Figure 3-24 to see how the strap should look.

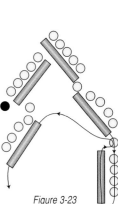

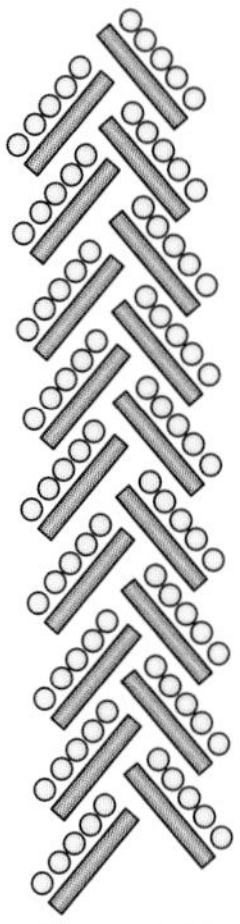

Figure 3-24

Right-Angle Weave Variations

The instructions for doing right-angle weave are covered on pages 18-20. The graphs shown here, along with the variations in the photo, are meant to give you ideas of how you can change the basic stitch to achieve a look you like to make a necklace or bracelet strap. All of the variations shown can be done in either method. The list of possibilities is endless. Experiment and enjoy!

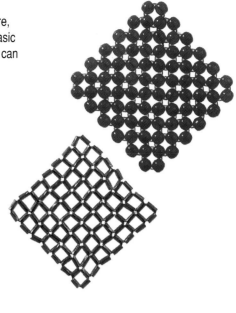

This variation is achieved by using the same size seed beads in two colors, placing the contrast color in the center of each weave pattern.

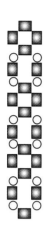

Use seed beads in one color and cube beads in another color to accomplish this variation.

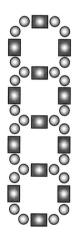

This variation also uses seed beads in one color and the cube beads in another, but instead of just one seed bead between each cube bead, there are two.

Use same-sized seed beads in two contrasting colors along with a bicone bead in a third color centered between stitch repeats.

Bugle beads in one color and seed beads in another work together in this variation.

This option is created with seed beads in two different sizes and colors, as well as barrel beads in yet another color.

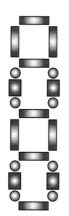

Use three different beads (bugle, seed, and cube beads) in two different colors for this unique chain. Note how one repeat is made up of bugles only, while the second repeat utilizes all three bead types.

Even a weave in all round beads can become interesting when sizes and colors are varied, as in this example.

THE FRINGE

Adding fringe to beaded jewelry can enhance the overall look and appeal of the finished piece. This is especially true of beaded cabochons and amulet bags. Fringe can be used anywhere you think you need it to decorate your item, though it is most commonly found at the bottom of the piece. Experiment and add it where you think it looks best.

Straight Fringe

To do a straight fringe, decide which beads you wish to use. They may be beads that you have already used in your piece or different ones in colors that match or contrast. Choose different sizes and shapes, as well as different colors. Lay out your beads and experiment with them until you have a pleasing pattern. Your fringe may be all the same length or vary by getting progressively longer until it comes to a point in the middle. Try alternating the lengths of the fringe or making it slant from one side to the other. If your piece has an uneven bottom, a straight fringe will be uneven also. Look at other projects to determine the kind of fringe you prefer. Here is how to incorporate straight fringe:

1 Secure a new thread in the worked part of your piece, close to where you want to start your fringe.

2 Come out between two beads and string on your beads in the order you want.

3 Skip the last bead (or more if you want a looped ending) and pass the thread back through all the beads to the top, as in Figure 3-25.

4 Go through the next bead to the left or right of where you started and repeat the fringe strand as in step 3. Be sure to pull the thread snugly.

Figure 3-25

Experiment with different bead combinations and patterns, as in the three illustrations shown here, to achieve variety in straight fringe.

Branched Fringe

Branched fringe is usually done with seed beads. It works well where you want a bushy-looking fringe, like on a beard or a botanical-themed piece.

1 Come out of your work and string on a number of beads. In this case, eight beads are used.

2 Referring to Figure 3-28, skip one bead and pass back through three, pulling the thread snug.

3 String on nine, skip one, and pass back through four.

4 String on 11, skip one, and pass back through five.

Tip

The number of beads given should change with each fringe you make. The idea of branched fringe is for it to look like branches, and branches vary in length.

5 String on seven, skip one, and pass back through all the beads in a row up the middle to the top, as in Figure 3-26.

6 Pass to the next bead and repeat.

Figure 3-26

34

Looped Fringe

Looped fringe is exactly what it says—looped. It can be used on all sorts of projects and looks best on the bottom or side of a piece.

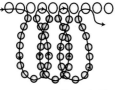

1 Referring to Figure 3-27, come out of the worked piece between two beads and string on the number of beads desired—in this case, 15 beads make up each loop. Remember, you need twice the number of beads to get the length.

Figure 3-27

2 Go into your piece one bead over from where you started and pass through that bead.

3 String on 15 more beads and repeat step 2. Continue in this manner until the fringe is complete.

Twisted Fringe

Twisted fringe takes a little time to master. This method works best with seed beads and can be used anywhere you would use a fringe.

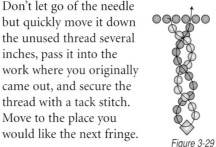

1 Thread on enough beads to get slightly longer than desired fringe length—in this example, 12 seed beads are strung—and follow with one or more decorative beads. Thread on an equal number of seed beads beyond the decorative beads (12 more). Push beads up tight against the work and needle up against last bead, as in Figure 3-28. Twist your needle around in a circular manner for several twists.

Figure 3-28

2 Hold the center decorative bead with your other hand while holding the needle tightly and match the two ends of the fringe. Let go of the decorative bead and the strand should twist around itself, as in Figure 3-29. Don't let go of the needle but quickly move it down the unused thread several inches, pass it into the work where you originally came out, and secure the thread with a tack stitch. Move to the place you would like the next fringe.

Figure 3-29

3 Repeat steps 1 and 2 until fringed edge is complete.

This Matchbox Necklace by Stella Maris of Fort Lauderdale, Florida, proves that you can make elegant jewelry out of things you would normally discard.

Linda Currier of Elsie Creations covers wooden spools with vividly colored bands of Peyote-stitched beads. Her creations are strung on necklaces of various fibers that complement her beaded spools.

While walking the hobby industry's trade show, I saw Sharon Wald of Making Tracks, Ink., a Montana rubber stamp company, demonstrating stamping on the pieces of glass and metal they produce. When I explained my "found" object project, she graciously offered me some of her samples to use. I created this brooch with one of her pieces.

BEADING A CABOCHON

Cabochon is the term used to refer to gemstones that are cut in a convex shape without facets. They have flat backs and domed fronts. When looking for found objects to use in jewelry, a gemstone cabochon is a good choice to start with. They are cut from semiprecious stones and come in a large variety of colors, sizes, and shapes. You can often find them in bead stores; however, rock shops and lapidary shows are better places to hunt.

Leopard Skin Agate Brooch

This beautiful brooch follows the step-by-step procedure for making a leather-backed cabochon, the most common way to encase a cabochon in beads. The cabochon is first glued to a piece of leather, Ultrasuede™, Lacy's Stiff Stuff™, or other stiff backing material. A beaded collar (bezel) is then built around the stone on this backing, and the decorative beads are couched in place around the collar. The excess leather is trimmed off so it doesn't show. Leather can be tough to work with, so be sure to stick your needle straight through the leather and not at an angle.

To begin:

1 Use the Gem-Tac™ and glue the cabochon to the center of the backing material, being sure to keep the glue away from the edge of the stone about ¹⁄₁₆". Be sparing with the glue so it won't ooze out under the edges of the gemstone. Allow glue to dry thoroughly.

2 Single-thread the needle with about 2 yards bead thread and tie a large knot at the end of the thread. Bring the needle up from under the fabric piece about a half-bead width from the stone and pull the thread through until knot is against the backing on the underside.

3 With the threaded needle, string on two black seed beads. Place beads against the stone in a line and take the needle back down through backing at the edge of the second bead in line with the bead hole, as shown below.

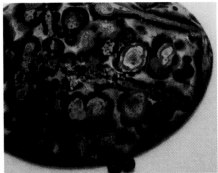

Step 3

4 Come up again in the first hole made, pass the needle back through the first two beads, and string on two more, as shown in the photo below.

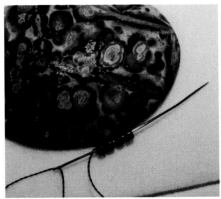

Step 4

5 Take the needle down through the backing against fourth bead. Come back up between the second and third beads, pass through the third and fourth beads again, and string on two more beads. This is backstitching. Refer to the backstitching instructions, page 25, for further assistance, if necessary.

6 Continue backstitching, as in step 5, around the cabochon until you get back to the beginning, as shown in both the photo and Figure 4-1. Try to fit an even number of beads around the stone.

Figure 4-1

Step 6

To make the collar:

1 Pass the needle through the first bead attached to the backing in the base row and bring it out between it and the next bead. String one bead on the needle, skip the next bead in the base row, and pass the needle through the following bead, as shown in the photo below.

Step 1

(continued)

Materials

- 40mm x 30mm leopard skin agate
- 5 grams black opaque 11° seed beads
- 2 grams red 11° seed beads
- 2 grams black matte 8° seed beads
- 2 grams black opaque 8° seed beads
- 40 black opaque 3mm x 4mm teardrop beads
- 2 red opaque 5mm round beads
- 2 black opaque 11mm x 5mm dagger beads
- 3" x 3½" piece Lacy's Stiff Stuff™
- 2¼" square piece black leather
- 1½" silver pin back
- Fabri-Tac™ Permanent Glue
- Nymo D beading thread
- Size 10 sharps needle
- Chalk pencil

Tip

When threading your bead needle, 2 yards is the suggested amount. However, if this is too much for you, cut it shorter. Just remember that the fewer times you have to change the thread, the better it is.

2 String on a second bead, skip the next bead in the base row, and take the needle through the following bead. Keep the thread tension tight. The beads you are adding should be sitting on top of the beads in the base row with a space between every bead, as in Figure 4-2.

Figure 4-2

3 Continue in the same manner as step 2 with picking up a bead, skipping one in the base row, and passing the thread through the next base-row bead until you have worked your way around the stone and get back to the beginning, as shown.

4 For the next row, add a bead between each second-row bead, just as in step 3 and as shown in Figure 4-3. You are now doing a peyote stitch around the cabochon.

Figure 4-3

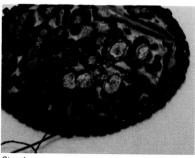

Step 4

5 Make several rows of peyote stitch, as in Figure 4-4, so that you have enough to come up over the curve of the stone.

Figure 4-4

6 Sort your beads and use the thinner ones in the top rows. Remember to keep your thread very snug. Go through the top row a second time, pulling securely after each bead to tighten and strengthen the top row. Work the thread to underside and tie off securely, as shown.

Step 6

To add embellishing beads:

1 Secure a new thread in the underside of the backing and bring the needle up at any point about a half-bead width from the completed collar (bezel).

2 Alternating red beads with black matte 8º beads, thread on enough beads to go completely around the collar and lay snugly against the base of the collar. Pass the needle through these beads again, and take the needle and the thread into the backing to secure.

3 Hold the ring of beads against the backing, referring to the couching instructions, page 26, if necessary, and begin to couch the ring of beads to the backing between every two beads, as shown, until you get back to the beginning.

Step 3

4 When couching is complete, carefully trim the excess backing material away from the piece so it is just slightly larger than the beaded oval. Be very careful not to cut any threads. Before doing the next step, use this oval backing as a pattern to cut the black leather needed for the final backing.

5 Sew teardrop black beads, alternating with opaque black 8º beads, around the edge to encircle the beaded piece.

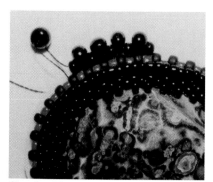

Steps 5 and 6

6 Bring a new thread up between the collar and the red-and-matte-black row of beads. Thread on enough black 11° seed beads to go around the collar above the red-black row. Pass through the beads again, making a ring, and couch in place. The beads lay against the collar and just above the red-black row, as shown.

To attach the pin back:

1 Place the pin backing centered on the upper inside back piece and mark both ends with chalk pencil.

2 Cut a small slit at both marks and insert pin back through so the bar part is against the inside of the leather, as shown below. Glue in place and set aside to dry.

Step 2

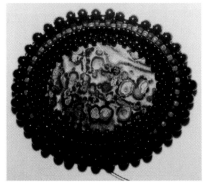

Front side after pin back is attached.

To make hanging loops:

1 Determine the center of one long side of the brooch (one of the teardrop beads could be your guide for finding center). Bring a new double-thread out of the edge of the piece one teardrop bead over from center.

2 Thread on two black seed beads, one red, three black, one red, one dagger bead, one red, three black, one red, and two black, as shown in Figure 4-5.

Figure 4-5

3 Take the needle into the backing three teardrop beads from where you started. Secure with a tack stitch. Then move over two teardrop beads from where the last stitch was secured and thread on beads in the sequence shown in Figure 4-6.

Figure 4-6

4 Take the needle in two teardrop beads over from the first loop. Secure by working the thread through the beading, tying half-knots as you work.

To finish:

1 Use the Fabri-Tac™ and glue the leather centered to the back of the piece. The pin back should be to the top, above the hanging loops.

Step 1

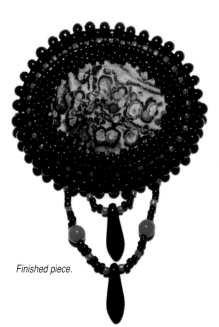

Finished piece.

41

Bronze Septarian Necklace

On the outside, Septarian gemstone is a nondescript gray nodule, but inside, the stones are lovely creamy-yellow crystal formations with a dark brown matrix—just perfect for jewelry. You will see the stone cut and polished and used as bookends or carved into fetishes with the open crystal center exposed. This necklace and the following two color variations combine different beads, straps, and fringe to get three different looks to show the possibilities of even a very limited color palette.

(First published in Jewelry Crafts Magazine)

1 Follow the basic instructions, pages 25 and 26, to mount your stone on backing and make the beaded collar. Do the collar with the metallic seed beads and use one row of matte for accent. Couch the outside beads in place as follows: first row in bronze metallic 8° seed beads; next row in the matte cream 8° seed beads, alternating with bronze metallic 11° seed beads (D-B-D-B, etc.); and the final row in bronze metallic 6mm bicones. Do not put leather back on yet.

2 Refer to the photo below to see bead-stringing pattern on fringe and where fringe is positioned on pendant. The fringe bead sequence is: A-C-A-C-A-C-A-C-A-C-E-C-D-F-D-C-E. Continue with A-B-A-G-A-B-A, skip these last seven beads and pass back up into the E-bead and through the rest of the fringe sequence to the top. Move to the next bead and repeat eight more times.

Step 2

3 Using the instructions from page 29, use the brown matte and bronze metallic seed beads to make a scalloped Peyote neckband long enough to go over your head. There is no clasp on this necklace. Refer to the charting in Figure 4-7 for the bead pattern on the neckband.

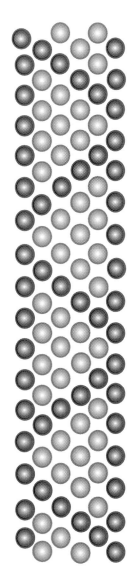
Figure 4-7

Materials
- 20 grams brown matte 11° seed beads (A)
- 20 grams bronze metallic 11° seed beads (B)
- 200 bronze metallic 8° seed beads (C)
- 100 matte cream 8° seed beads (D)
- 47 bronze metallic 6mm bicones (E)
- 9 bronze metallic 6mm round faceted beads (F)
- 9 bronze 11mm x 5mm dagger beads (G)
- Brown or black leather (1" larger than stone all around)
- Brown Silamide thread
- Size 10 sharps needle

Bead Key

 A

 B

 C

 D

E

 F

G

Root Beer Septarian Necklace

A variation of the Bronze Septarian Necklace, this piece uses
root beer-colored beads and branched fringe to complement the
stone and provide a different look.

1 Refer to the basic instructions on pages 25 and 26 for mounting a stone on leather and doing a beaded collar. Bead it with the matte beads and an occasional row of the root beer beads. Do the last row with the root beer 14° seed beads.

2 Couch one row of the root beer 8° seed beads around the beaded collar.

3 Make a ring of cream 11° seed beads and place it around the collar and above the couched row. Then, couch the cream-colored row in place. Trim the leather.

4 Bring the needle up between two of the 8° beads on the lower left corner of the outer ring. Referring to Figure 4-8, string on two root beer 11° beads, one brown matte 11°, and one root beer 11°, pass back through the matte 11° bead, and string on two more root beer 11° beads. Take the needle down into the bead to the right of where you came up and pass through that bead to the left. Pass through the next two beads and come up, as shown. Repeat the process until you get to the lower right corner. You are actually making loops around the outer edge, though they will look like points.

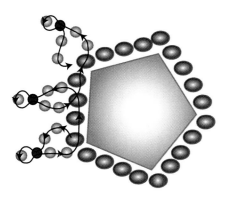

Figure 4-8

5 Make the fringe in the beading pattern as shown in Figure 4-9. It is a variation of branched fringe. Do a fringe between every bead on the bottom outer ring.

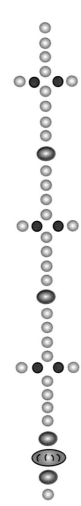

Figure 4-9

6 To make the necklace strap, follow the spiral rope instructions, page 31. The core beads are dark brown matte 11° beads and the outer beads are root beer 11° beads.

7 When the spiral rope strap is the desired length, attach at upper corners of the beaded cabochon by stitching through the rope into the edge of the beaded cabochon until it feels secure.

Materials

- 30 grams root beer aurora borealis 11° seed beads (A)
- 10 grams dark brown matte 11° seed beads (B)
- 1 gram cream translucent aurora borealis 11° seed beads
- 1 gram root beer aurora borealis 14° seed beads
- 150 root beer aurora borealis 8° seed beads (C)
- 15 bronze 3mm x 6mm rondelle beads (D)
- Brown Silamide thread
- Brown leather (1" larger than stone all around)
- Size 10 sharps needle

Bead Key

○ A
● B
◯ C
⦅ ( ) ⦆ D

45

Tip

When determining the spiral rope strap length in step 7, be sure to make the necklace long enough to go over your head or do a shorter piece on each side and attach a clasp.

Potawatomi Septarian Necklace

The use of these particular beads results in a more modern-
looking piece than what was created in either of the previous
two Septarian necklaces. The lines here are clean and sleek.

1 Follow the basic directions on pages 25 and 26 for mounting the stone and doing a beaded collar. Use matte khaki brown 11º beads for most of the collar. Use an accent row of the antique gold and then one or two rows of the silver-lined brown 14º beads to end.

2 Make the first couched row with 11º antique gold beads, alternating with 8º matte khaki brown beads. The outside couched row is the antique gold cube beads. Lay a ring of antique gold 11º beads between the collar and on top of the first couched row, and couch them in place.

3 Refer to the instructions on page 35 for making twisted fringe and do one across the bottom approximately 13 strands wide. Each fringe strand is made by threading 35 khaki brown 11º beads, one gold disk, and 35 gold 11º seed beads. The more you twist the needle, the tighter the twist will be on the fringe.

4 For the strap, refer to the Potawatomi weave instructions, page 30, to make the band with both the gold and khaki brown 11º seed beads.

5 Once the woven strap is long enough to go over your head, attach it to the beaded cabochon at the upper corners by stitching through the strap into the edge of the cabochon until it feels secure. Refer to the project photograph on previous page for placement.

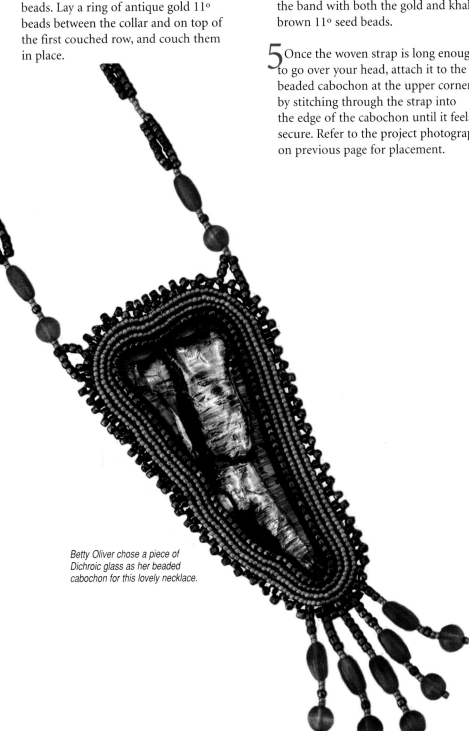

Betty Oliver chose a piece of Dichroic glass as her beaded cabochon for this lovely necklace.

Materials

- 20 grams matte khaki brown 11º seed beads
- 20 grams antique gold 11º seed beads
- 1 gram silver-lined brown 14º seed beads
- 33 matte khaki brown 8º seed beads
- 44 antique gold 4mm cube beads
- 13 antique gold 2mm x 6mm disk spacer beads
- 2 3" squares brown leather
- Brown Silamide thread
- Size 10 sharps needle

Marble Moon Man Necklace

Inspiration for this necklace came from the piece of Picasso marble that is the figure's body. When I found the carved bone face cabochon, the two just seemed to meld together into a unique figure.

1 Center the piece of marble on the leather with the head cabochon about ⅛" above it. Glue the piece of marble in place with the gem glue. Put the head aside and let the glue dry completely.

2 Follow directions for the Leopard Agate Brooch, steps 2 (to begin) through step 6 (collar) on pages 39 and 40, to bead around the marble body cabochon, but use three 14° beads instead of two in the base row. Try to fit in an even number of beads. If the face cabochon is thinner than the body marble piece, glue some extra layers of felt to even it up. Glue the face in place above the body and make the collar.

3 After the face collar is complete, come up from underneath the piece with a new thread at the point where the head meets the body—either side will do. String one brown translucent 8° seed bead on the needle and alternate with black opaque 6° seed beads to thread on enough beads to encircle the body. Pass the thread back through all the beads again to strengthen. Couch between each bead.

4 Come up at the same spot as where you began step 3 and thread on enough brown-lined amber 11° seed beads to encircle the body but not the neck. Pass the thread back through all the beads. Couch these beads in place between every two to three beads.

5 Come up at the neck and thread on enough amber 11° seed beads to cover neck. Make a tack stitch and pass the thread back through the beads to strengthen.

6 To make headdress, thread on 11 ecru opaque leaf beads, alternating with amber 11° seed beads. Pull beaded thread snugly around head and couch in place on both sides of each leaf bead.

7 Thread on enough brown translucent 8° seed beads to encircle head. Couch these in place over the ends of the leaf beads, taking stitches where you can.

8 Using a sharp scissors, trim away excess leather being very careful not to cut any of the threads. Place second piece of leather behind beaded piece, wrong sides together. Carefully cut out the backing piece, using the beaded piece as a pattern. Set aside.

Finished head.

For the fringe:

1 With a new thread, bring the needle up through the backing in the center bottom of the piece. Secure the thread and come out on the top just under the black/brown row of beads around the body.

2 Referring to Figure 4-10, thread on beads as shown for the center fringe only.

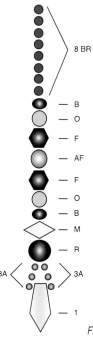

8 BR

— B
— O
— F
— AF
— F
— O
— B
— M
— R

3A   3A

— 1

Figure 4-10

(continued)

Materials

-O- ⅞"-diameter carved bone face cabochon

-O- 2-¾" x 1" Picasso marble cabochon

-O- 5 grams matte gunmetal gray 14° seed beads

-O- 5 grams brown-lined amber 11° seed beads (A)

-O- 100 black opaque 6° seed beads (B)

-O- 160 brown translucent 8° seed beads (BR)

-O- 26 ecru opaque 11mm x 5mm leaf beads (L)

-O- 87 black opaque 7mm round beads (R)

-O- 35 beige fluted matte translucent 5mm x 7mm bicone beads (M)

-O- 30 ecru opaque 5mm faceted round beads (O)

-O- 30 black opaque 6mm faceted round beads (F)

-O- 17 amber translucent 6mm faceted round beads (AF)

-O- 4 ecru opaque 12mm x 6mm cone beads (C)

-O- 2 ecru opaque 9mm x 7mm oval beads (OV)

-O- 4 black opaque 10mm round beads (BO)

-O- 3" x 6" piece black Ultrasuede™ or leather

-O- 1½" x 4" piece black Ultrasuede™ or leather

-O- ¾" x 3½" piece plastic or plastic canvas

-O- Gold toggle clasp

-O- 2 gold clamshell bead tips

-O- 2 small crimp beads

-O- Gem-Tac™ Glue or other gem glue

-O- Fabri-Tac™ Fabric Glue

-O- 2"-square scrap white felt or leather

-O- Black Silamide bead thread

-O- 2 yards Spiderwire™ 6 lb. test fishing line

-O- Size 10 sharps needle

49

3 Skip the last three amber 11° seed beads and pass the needle back through all the beads to the top. Make a tack stitch to hold.

4 Take the needle a half brown bead's width to one side or the other of center and come out to the front.

5 Thread on seven brown translucent 8° seed beads and repeat the Figure 4-10 pattern.

6 Repeat steps 2 through 5 until you have seven fringe on either side of center, decreasing the brown beads at the top by one bead each time until you have three brown beads only. The last two fringe on each side move up the lower sides of the body.

7 Secure all threads with knots and glue.

Finished fringe section.

For the arms:

1 Use gem glue to attach the piece of plastic up the back of the body to strengthen it. Let dry.

2 Bring a double-threaded needle out from the back at the shoulder. Thread on one brown translucent 8° seed bead, two cone beads, two ecru oval beads, two cone beads, and one brown translucent 8° seed bead (BR-C-C-OV-OV-C-C-BR). Be sure the wide part of the cone beads point toward the oval beads. Take the thread through the other shoulder and secure in back.

3 Repeat steps 1 and 2 for the other arm.

Finished arms.

For the neck strap:

1 Double-thread your needle with the Spiderwire and tie a crimp bead at the very end of the Spiderwire. Make several knots against the crimp bead and glue. Trim the ends close.

2 Thread on a clamshell bead tip so it cups over the crimp bead and use smooth-jawed pliers to close the clamshell.

3 As shown in Figure 4-11, thread on the following sequence of beads: A-A-A-BR-B-R-M-R-B-BR. Skip the first three A-beads and repeat the remaining pattern (BR-B-R-M-R-B-BR) seven more times—making eight total patterns.

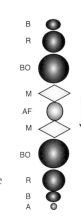
Figure 4-11

4 Thread on the following sequence of beads, as shown in Figure 4-12: B-R-BO-M-AF-M-BO-R-B-A. Pull the beads up so no thread shows and secure the thread with a tack stitch. Work the needle to the other side of the head through the beading.

Figure 4-12

5 Bring the thread out at the same point on the other side of the head. Thread on beads in reverse order as you did in steps 3 and 4.

6 Take the thread through a clamshell tip and a crimp bead. Secure as you did for the other end of the necklace.

7 Attach the clamshell tips to the clasp.

8 Use fabric glue to attach the leather backing piece to the back of the beaded cabochon head and body.

Amethyst Crystal Necklace

This slice of amethyst geode was a must-have for me. The piece did pose a number of serious obstacles, however. Since it is translucent, a solid background would have hidden a lot of the beauty, so I had to come up with an alternative to the leather backing used on the Septarian necklaces. This necessitated a beading technique that would be secure and still let light get to it from all angles. I think the configuration I settled on is very pleasing.

1 Single-thread your needle with about 1 yard of thread and string on 36 lavender seed beads.

2 Pass the needle back through the beads again and pull them into a ring. Tie a square-knot to secure the ring.

3 String on three lavender seed beads and go back into the ring two beads away from where you started. Continue around the ring in this manner, making loops of beads, as shown in Figure 4-13.

Figure 4-13

4 Place the ring on the amethyst slab. You may need to adjust your bead pattern, depending on your piece.

5 For the second row, string on three lavender seed beads between every point bead of the first row, as shown in Figure 4-14.

Figure 4-14

6 For the third row, string on two crystal beads between every point bead of the second row, as in Figure 4-15.

Figure 4-15

7 For the next row, string on one lavender seed between each of crystal beads in the third row, as in Figure 4-16.

Figure 4-16

8 For the final row, string on three lavender seed beads between each point bead of the previous row, as shown in Figure 4-17.

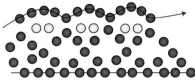

Figure 4-17

9 To hold the band on the amethyst slab, make a strap on each side of the piece, as shown in the photo. Alternate three lavender seed beads with one crystal seed bead. Choose places where there is a natural dip in the top of the stone so the bands will hold. Secure the thread ends in the work.

For the neckband:

1 Single-thread your needle with about 4 feet of thread.

2 Secure the thread in the top of the side of the woven band.

3 The neckband is a modified daisy stitch. Referring to Figure 4-18 for guidance, come out between two of the three top beads. String on six lavender seed beads and one amethyst 6mm bead. Pass back through the top bead to the right of where you started. String on six more seed beads and take them around the 6mm amethyst center bead and back through the sixth seed bead of the first pick-up.

4 Follow the thread path in Figure 4-18 and alternate two amethyst beads in the center with one crystal bead until you have 45 large beads. You will end with two amethyst beads.

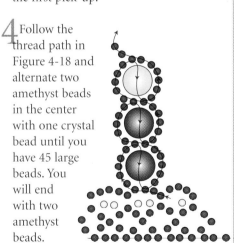

Figure 4-18

52

Materials

- ⦾ 2½" x 2¼" pie-shaped slice of amethyst geode
- ⦾ 72 amethyst gemstone 6mm round beads
- ⦾ 4 amethyst gemstone 11mm x 6mm oval beads
- ⦾ 30 crystal aurora borealis 6mm faceted beads
- ⦾ 10 grams 11° lavender silver-lined seed beads
- ⦾ 10 grams 11° crystal aurora borealis silver-lined seed beads
- ⦾ Silver toggle clasp
- ⦾ 2 silver clamshell bead tips
- ⦾ 2 silver 5mm split rings
- ⦾ White Nymo D thread
- ⦾ Size 10 bead needle

5 Finish end with a clamshell bead tip and attach the clasp.

6 Repeat steps 2 through 5 for the other side.

Finishing the piece:

1 Starting at the necklace band on the side, do a band of right-angle weave around the middle of the amethyst slab, catching the edge of the necklace and the shoulder straps as you progress around the piece. Refer to photo below for guidance.

Step 1

2 Do a band of right-angle weave from the tops of the stone over to the shoulder straps. Refer to photo for placement.

Step 2

3 Do four dangles at the bottom of the piece with the oval amethyst beads, as shown in the accompanying photo.

Step 3

53

You can see that it is possible to find amethyst stone slabs cut similarly in size and shape to the one used for this necklace.

Imperial Jasper
Necklace and Earrings

This cabochon is framed with a modified daisy stitch and
horizontal netting. The bead weaving is all that secures the stone.
It is a little tricky to get it to fit just right, but the results are well
worth the effort.

1 Tie a stop bead on the end of your single-thread.

2 Refer to Figure 4-19 for the weaving pattern vertically. Using the bicones and the brown seed beads, string on eight seed beads, one bicone, and eight more seed beads.

3 Still referring to Figure 4-19, pass the needle back through the last brown seed bead of the first eight you picked up, pull the thread snugly, and string on seven seed beads and one bicone.

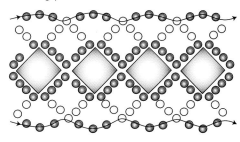

Figure 4-19

4 Pass the needle through the first of the second set of eight seed beads you did in the last pass. String on seven seed beads and go through the last bead of the first set of seven. Continue in this manner, which is a modified daisy stitch, until you have enough woven to fit around the outside edge of the cabochon tightly. Weave the two ends together.

5 Referring to Figure 4-20, which shows the beading pattern horizontally, string on five white seed beads between the two brown side beads of each pattern. Do this on both sides and secure the threads.

6 String on three brown seed beads and pass the needle through the center bead of the five white ones for each pattern repeat, on one side only, as shown in Figure 4-21. (Note: The figure shows both sides of the finished weave.) Go back around the circle, pull the thread snugly, and tie it off.

Figure 4-21

7 Place beaded piece on cabochon so the tightest side is on the back of the cabochon and then place it on a hard surface. Repeat the three-bead section as in step 6 on the top of the cabochon. Pull up as tightly as you can and secure the thread.

For the necklace strap:

1 Cut 2 yards of thread and place a needle on each end, making sure the ends are even. Thread a crimp bead on one needle. Pass both needles through a clamshell bead tip and center. Close the clamshell around the crimp bead.

(continued)

Materials ░░░░░░░░░░░░░░░░░░░░

-o- 48mm round Imperial Jasper cabochon

-o- 46 rose 7.5mm bicone beads

-o- 10 grams milk chocolate (brown) 11° seed beads

-o- 10 grams white pearl 11° seed beads

-o- Gold earring findings

-o- 4 gold clamshell bead tips

-o- 2 gold split rings

-o- Gold clasp

-o- Brown Nymo D bead thread

-o- Size 10 or 12 beading needle

55

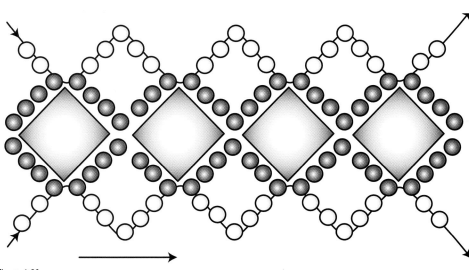

Figure 4-20

2 Referring to Figure 4-22, begin weaving the necklace by taking both needles through one brown seed bead. Thread a white seed bead on each needle. Pass each needle through one brown seed bead from opposite directions and pull snugly.

3 Pick up a white seed bead on each needle and pass both through one brown seed bead from opposite directions. Repeat once more.

4 Pick up three brown seed beads on each needle and one bicone on one needle. Pass the second needle through the bicone from the opposite direction.

5 Pick up three brown seed beads on one needle and four on the other. Pass first needle through the last brown bead on the second needle, from the opposite direction, and pull snugly.

6 Repeat the pattern doing three brown-white patterns and one bicone to desired length. The sample is 15 bicones long. End with the seed bead pattern.

7 Determine the top of the cabochon and pass both needles from the woven strap through a bicone. String on two chocolate seed beads and pass through the next bicone. Repeat until you have exited the fourth bicone.

8 Weave second half of necklace, starting with the seed bead pattern. Tie off the other end and attach a clamshell bead tip, a crimp bead, and the clasp.

For the earrings:

1 Cut an 8" to 10" length of thread and place a needle on each end. Thread on seven brown seed beads and center them on the thread.

2 String on one bicone, pass each needle through from opposite directions, and pull the thread snugly.

3 String four brown seed beads on one needle and three brown seed beads on the second needle. Pass the second needle through the fourth bead on the other side.

4 Alternate white and brown seed beads and weave, as in the left-most portion of Figure 4-22. Do three patterns.

5 Thread on a clamshell bead tip from the outside in and add a crimp bead. Tie off the threads against the crimp bead. Glue knot, trim, and close the clamshell. Attach to earring finding.

6 Repeat steps 1 through 5 for other earring.

56

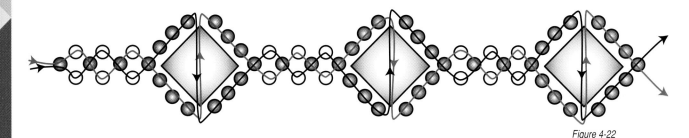

Figure 4-22

Fluorite Slab Necklace

This slab of fluorite is not actually a cabochon since it is not domed. It has straight sides and is thick and heavy. Fluorite has fractures, inclusions, and subtle color changes that are best seen when light passes through. I decided to bead around this piece of fluorite in right-angle weave with 11º and 14º seed beads. You may choose to vary your piece by beading the woven collar in Peyote stitch instead.

1 Referring to the instructions on pages 18-20 and using silver-lined green 11° seed beads, complete a right-angle weave band that is one pattern too short to go around your particular stone. Do enough rows so that the weaving is not quite as wide as the stone is thick. Join the ends as shown in the basic right-angle weave instructions.

2 Change to the lavender 14° beads and weave several rows on one side of the green woven piece. Do one row of lavender weave on the other side as well. Place stone inside the woven band and continue making rows with the lavender beads until you have the stone secured.

3 Determine which side you would like for the top edge of the piece and imbed a new doubled thread in the green part of the band close to the side of the top, as shown in Figure 4-23. Hold the piece horizontally and bring the needle out of the top green vertical bead in the row you have chosen.

4 Referring to the bead key, string on beads in the following sequence: GS-GS-GS-D-R-D-GS-GS-GS.

5 Moving in the direction away from the top of the slab, skip over to the third row of vertical beads from the row where you started (row 1) and go to the other side of the band (bottom as you are holding the piece). Pass the needle through the vertical beads in that row from bottom to top, as shown in Figure 4-24, and pull up. The beads you threaded on should be sitting at an angle to the band.

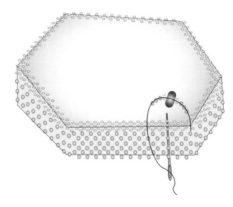

Figure 4-24

6 String on another set of beads as in step 4 and repeat step 5. Continue in this manner all the way around to the other side of the piece to the top. Do not place beads across the top.

Materials

- 2" x 4" fluorite slab
- 20 fluorite 8mm x 6mm tube beads (T)
- 47 fluorite 6mm x 8mm rondelles (R)
- 74 flat gold 4mm-diameter disk beads (D)
- 10 grams silver-lined green 11° seed beads (GS)
- 5 grams silver-lined lavender 14° seed beads (LS)
- 12 gold 4mm round fluted metal beads (F)
- Gold toggle clasp
- 2 gold split rings
- 2 gold clamshell bead tips
- Nymo D white thread
- Size 10 beading needle

Bead Key

▢	T
▢	R
▭	D
○	GS
○	LS
○	F

58

Figure 4-23 (front view)

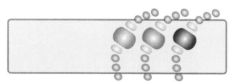

(side view)

For the neck strap:

1 Double-thread your needle and secure the thread in the weave you completed around the fluorite slab. Bring it out at the back top corner of the piece.

2 Referring to Figure 4-25, string on beads in the following sequence: GS-GS-F-R-GS-D-T-D-GS-R-GS-D-T-D-GS-R-F.

3 Skip the first two green seed beads, and repeat pattern F-R-GS-D-T-D-GS-R-GS-D-T-D-GS-R-F four more times.

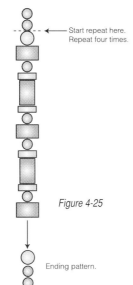

← Start repeat here. Repeat four times.

Figure 4-25

Ending pattern.

4 Finish the strand with one gold disk and one green seed bead.

5 Tie off the strand and finish with a clamshell bead tip, a crimp bead, and the clasp.

6 Repeat steps 1 through 5 for the other strap side.

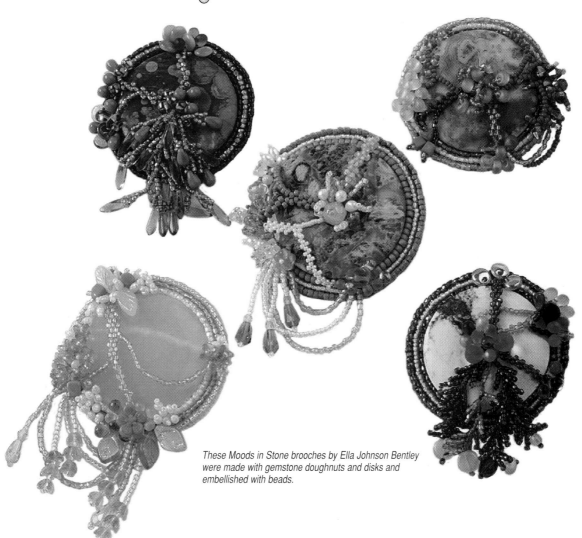

These Moods in Stone brooches by Ella Johnson Bentley were made with gemstone doughnuts and disks and embellished with beads.

Magnifying Glass Necklace

My husband suggested I make a necklace out of this magnifying glass I found so I would have it handy whenever I needed it. In experimenting with it, I realized it was the same thickness as a #1 bugle is long. A bugle bead ladder seemed to be the answer. Netting around the front and back edges holds the glass firmly in place.

1 Referring to the instructions for making a bugle bead ladder on page 21 and using the purple iris bugles, make a ladder long enough to go around the magnifying glass and join it together. Try to end up with a ladder that contains a total number of beads that is divisible by three.

2 Come out one bugle bead and string on two purple 11° seed beads, one gold 11° seed bead, and two more purple 11° seed beads. The bead sequence is therefore P11-P11-G-P11-P11.

3 Skip the next bugle in the ladder and go down to the third one, making a loop with the seed beads, as shown in Figure 4-26.

Figure 4-26

4 On the other side of the ladder, take the needle into the next bugle and come back to the first side.

5 Repeat steps 2 through 4 around the ladder.

6 When looping is completed on one side of the ladder, repeat steps 2 through 5 on the other side, using the bead holes you didn't use on the first pass.

7 On one side of the looped ladder (for the backside of the magnifying glass), string on two gold beads between each gold bead of the loops, as shown in Figure 4-27, and pull the thread snugly.

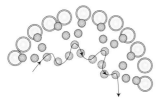

Figure 4-27

8 Secure the thread and cut off the end.

9 Repeat steps 7 and 8 on the side of the looped ladder (for the front side of the magnifying glass), but before you pull the beading up, insert the glass. Then, pull the thread snugly and secure it as before.

10 On the front side, bring the threaded needle up through the bugle between one loop, string on a purple 8° seed bead, and bring the needle back down the same bugle, as shown in Figure 4-28.

Figure 4-28

11 Weave in and out of the bugles to the next loop and repeat step 10 all the way around the piece.

For the neck straps:

1 Cut 1 yard of filament and single-thread the needle.

2 Tie a crimp bead on the end and string on a clamshell from the inside.

3 String on one gold, one purple 8°, one purple 6°, one purple 8°, and repeat this pattern (G-P8-P6-P8) for about 16". End with a gold bead.

4 Alternate purple 8° seed beads with purple 6° seed beads (P8-P6-P8-P6) for 2".

5 String on two purple 11° seed beads, one gold, two more purple 11° seed beads (P11-P11-G-P11-P11) and pass through a bugle on the original ladder. On the other side of the bugle, repeat the same five beads as before (P11-P11-G-P11-P11).

6 Pass the needle back through the entire strand to the beginning, tie off the thread end against the crimp bead, glue knot, trim threads, close the clamshell, and attach the clasp.

7 Repeat steps 1 through 3.

8 Pass the needle through existing 2" strand that was created in step 4.

9 Repeat steps 5 and 6.

Materials

- 30mm-diameter round magnifying glass
- 51 matte purple iris #1 (5mm) bugle beads (B)
- 102 matte purple iris 6° seed beads (P6)
- 250 matte purple iris 8° seed beads (P8)
- 2 grams matte purple iris 11° seed beads (P11)
- 2 grams gold metal-plated 11° seed beads (G)
- Gold toggle clasp
- 2 gold clamshell bead tips
- 2 gold jump rings
- Gray fine braided filament thread
- Size 10 or 12 beading needle

Painted Stone Doughnut Necklace

While wandering around a lapidary show, I happened to find several painted stone doughnuts. I was familiar with gemstone doughnuts, but I had never seen any like these with their beautiful colors and designs. The vendor said they came from Peru.

1 Single-thread your needle with a yard of thread.

2 Referring to the instructions on page 32 for making a herringbone chain, weave three patterns in each of the five colors of seed beads (with black bugles), repeat, and then end the strand with patterns of the beginning color. In the sample shown, the strand begins with three red repeats, followed by three amber, three light blue, three lavender, and three turquoise. Then, the whole pattern repeats again (red, amber, light blue, lavender, and turquoise) and ends with three red.

3 Finish the strand with a clamshell bead tip, a crimp bead, and the clasp.

4 Repeat steps 1 through 3 for the other side of the neck strap.

5 Work a short thread (10") into the end of the strand that does not have the clasp and bring the needle out the last section of seed beads.

6 String on enough 11° black seed beads to go around doughnut (through the center hole) and take the needle back into the other set of seed beads, as shown in Figure 4-29.

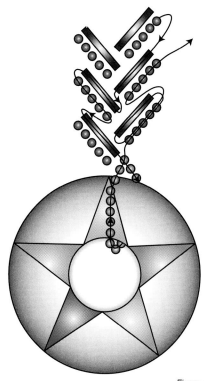

Figure 4-29

7 Work the thread through the piece and back through the black seed beads once more. Secure the thread end with a knot in beaded band.

8 Repeat steps 5 through 7 for the other side of the neck strap.

Materials
- Painted stone doughnut
- 2 grams each 11° seed beads
  - black
  - five additional colors to match doughnut
- 136 black 6mm bugle beads
- 2 black 8° seed beads
- Gold clasp
- 2 gold clamshell tips
- 2 gold split rings
- 2 small crimp beads
- Gray or black fine braided filament line
- Size 10 or 12 beading needle

63

Peruvian painted stone doughnuts and seed beads come together to give this finished piece a Southwestern flair.

This lovely creation by Elisa Cossey features a piece of jasper encased in an open-backed beaded cage.

Sigrid Wynn Evans used Peyote beading around cabochons to make these playful beaded doll pins. Note the branched fringe hair.

DJ Levine uses stone doughnuts to make her doughnut ties. Strands of beads are tied around the doughnut piece in a Lark's head knot.

WEARABLE HARDWARE

Chapter 5

The hardware or home improvement store can be a treasure trove for the adventurous beader. There are all kinds of small parts and pieces that can be coupled with beads to make striking and unusual jewelry. In fact, there are so many interesting things that you won't know what to purchase first!

Drawer-Pull Lariat

This green German glass drawer-pull was extremely expensive, and if it were actually going to end up on a drawer, it would have never gone home with me! A necklace, however, is a totally different matter. The drawer-pull knob makes a great knot for this lariat necklace. If you don't like things that are tight around your throat, then try this faux lariat. It maintains its shape without choking you.

1 Double-thread your needle so you have 24". Secure the end with a crimp bead and a clamshell tip.

2 Referring to Figure 5-1, string on bead sequence F-E-D and then alternate the green 8º seed beads with the bronze pearls (E-D-E-D) until you have about 16". End the beading sequence with a green 8º seed bead and bronze 11º seed bead (E-F). Finish the strand with a clamshell tip and a crimp bead. Set aside.

Figure 5-1

3 Do a row of right-angle weave with the bronze 11º seed beads that is long enough to go around the neck of the drawer-pull. Place around the drawer-pull and tie off. Knot, glue, and bury your thread tails in the work. Set aside.

4 Single-thread the needle with about 5 feet of thread. String a bronze 11º seed bead, alternating with a green 8º seed bead, until you have six bronze and five green (F-E-F-E-F-E-F-E-F-E-F). Remove the thread from the needle and center the beads.

5 Rethread the needle with both ends of the thread and string on beads in the sequence shown in Figure 5-2 (E-F-C-F-A-F-C-F-E-D-E-D-E-D-E-F-C-F-A-F-C-F-E-D-E-D-E-D-E-F-C-B). String on the drawer-pull.

Figure 5-2

6 Thread on beads in the sequence illustrated in Figure 5-3 (A-F-C-F-E-D-E-D-E-D-E-F-C-F). Repeat this pattern twice more.

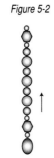

Figure 5-3

7 Thread on one green oval bead, one bronze 11º seed bead, one green faceted bead, one bronze 11º seed bead (A-F-C-F).

8 To finish this strand, alternate green 8º seed beads with bronze pearls (E-D-E-D) until you have 21 E's and 20 D's. End the strand with one F. Finish with a crimp bead and a clamshell tip.

9 For the second strand, repeat step 4.

10 Rethread the needle with both strands and string on beads in the sequence shown in Figure 5-4 (E-D-E-D-E-D-E-F-C-F-A-F-C-F-E-D-E-D-E-D-E-F-C).

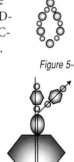

Figure 5-4

11 Pass the needle through the green roller bead and the drawer-pull of the first strand and the first green oval bead on other end of drawer-pull, as shown in Figure 5-5.

Figure 5-5

12 For the remainder of the strand, repeat steps 6 through 8.

13 Attach each clamshell tip to a jump ring.

14 Attach clamshells from short strand to jump rings.

15 Attach jump rings to the clasp.

Materials

- 27mm x 24mm green glass drawer-pull
- 10 green 11mm x 9mm oval beads (A)
- Green roller bead (B)
- 22 green aurora borealis fire-polished 6mm faceted beads (C)
- 125 bronze 6mm pearls (D)
- 149 green aurora borealis 8º seed beads (E)
- 100 bronze metallic 11º seed beads (F)
- Gold toggle clasp
- 4 gold clamshell bead tips
- 2 gold 4mm jump rings
- 4 small crimp beads
- Heavy beading thread to match beads
- Size 10 beading needle

Bead Key

- A
- B
- C
- D
- E
- F

Detail of finished center piece and dangle.

Heavy-Metal Necklace

We think these metal pieces are music box keys and most
everyone who saw them agreed with that assumption.
They make an interesting piece of jewelry to wear for
a special occasion—like a heavy-metal music concert.

1 Cut 2½ yards of bead thread and place a needle on each end.

2 Thread a crimp bead on one needle, center on the thread, and pass one needle through the crimp bead several times. Tie the threads in a secure knot around the bead.

3 Pass both needles through a clamshell tip from the inside and close clamshell around the crimp bead.

4 Pass both needles through one silver 11° seed bead.

5 Separate needles and then string three silver 11° seed beads on each needle.

6 Referring to the instructions for doing a double-needle ladder stitch on page 21, use a seed bead on each end of a bugle bead to work a strip 12 bugle beads long, as shown in Figure 5-6. Be sure to alternate shiny and matte black bugle beads, starting with a shiny one.

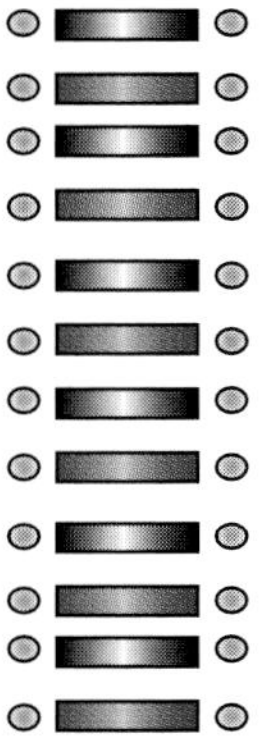

Figure 5-6

7 After you have completed the first section of 12 bugles, pass through one silver 11° seed bead, one black cube bead, and one silver 11° seed bead on each side, as shown in Figure 5-7.

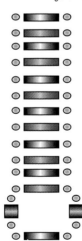

Figure 5-7

8 Repeat steps 4 through 7, as illustrated in Figure 5-8, until there are five sections.

9 Make a sixth 12-bead section, loop the section around a music box key, and take the last bead of the 12-bead section around to the first bead. Join the two together so that the key is secured on the strand by the beaded loop.

10 Work threads back through the beading, knot, and glue to secure the threads. Bury the tails in the work.

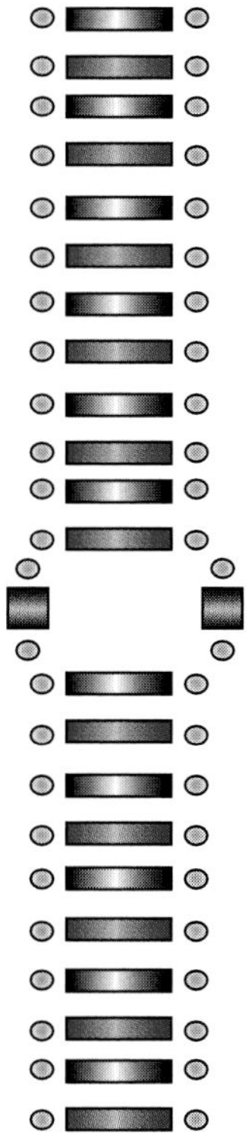

11 Repeat steps 1 through 10 for the other side of the neck strand.

12 With new thread, make a 12-bead section, loop the section around a music box key at the end of one of your worked pieces, and then through one of the remaining keys. Secure the ends of beading together.

13 Repeat step 12 for the other side of the neck strand.

14 Make two more 12-bead sections and attach the remaining keys, using the looping method to chain both sides of the neck strand together.

15 Attach the clasp to the split rings and bend a clamshell bar around the split rings with a round nose pliers.

Figure 5-8

Materials

- 5 music box keys
- 96 black #2 (6mm) bugle beads
- 96 matte black #2 (6mm) bugle beads
- 440 silver metallic 11° seed beads
- 20 matte black 3.5mm cube beads
- Silver toggle clasp
- 2 silver 5mm split rings
- 2 silver clamshell bead tips
- 2 small crimp beads
- Black Nymo D beading thread
- 2 size 10 beading needles
- Gem-Tac™ Permanent Adhesive

Tip

The instructions are given using the double-needle ladder method, but you can make it in the single-needle method, which is detailed on page 21, as well.

Key-Plate Necklace

During a trip, we happened on a shop that specialized in reproductions of old housing hardware. That's where I found this brass key-plate. It needed a few holes to make it work as a pendant, so I got out my handy drill and made them. The result is an interesting piece.

For the front dangles:

1 Drill holes in the upper corners and sides of key-plate, as shown in the photo.

Step 1

2 Double-thread your needle and make a knot on the very end.

3 String on one gold 11º seed bead and a gold disk and then bring the needle through a side hole on the plate from back to front.

4 Using the bead key, thread on beads in the sequence illustrated in Figure 5-9 (D-C-C-C-C-C-D-C-C-C-C-C-B-A-B-C-E-C-B-A-B-C-C-C-C-C-D-C-C-C-C-C-D).

Figure 5-9

5 Take the needle through to the back and string on one gold disk and one gold 11º seed bead. Bring the thread back around the gold 11º seed bead at the end and pass back through the beaded strand to strengthen. Tie off end in the beading.

6 Repeat the process of drilling holes, but this time, do so on either side of the keyhole.

7 Repeat steps 2 and 3.

8 Thread on beads in the sequence shown in Figure 5-10 (B-D-C-C-C-D-A-D), bring the thread back around the last gold 11º seed bead and pass back through the lavender/gold cathedral bead as shown in the same illustration, and then thread beads for the remainder of the dangle strand (D-C-C-C-D-B).

Figure 5-10

9 Bring the needle through to the back of the key-plate and finish as in step 5.

For the neck strap:

1 Double-thread the needle for a thread length of about 15".

2 At the end, thread on a crimp bead and a clamshell tip.

3 Alternate gold round beads with lavender/gold cathedral beads (B-A-B-A) until you have 17 repeats. Follow with one more gold round bead (B) and finish the end with a crimp bead and a clamshell tip.

4 Repeat steps 1 through 3 for the other strand.

5 Attach one end of each strand to the key-plate with a jump ring.

6 Attach the jump ring to the other end of each strand and attach the clasp.

Materials

- Brass key-plate
- 37 lavender/gold 10mm x 8mm cathedral beads (A)
- 42 gold 4mm round fluted beads (B)
- 26 purple luster 11º seed beads (C)
- 8 gold 11º seed beads (D)
- 16mm x 5mm gold dagger bead (E)
- 4 gold disk beads (F)
- 4 gold clamshell bead tips
- 4 small crimp beads
- 4 gold jump rings
- Gold clasp
- Gray braided filament line
- Size 10 bead needle
- Gem glue
- Drill and 1/64" drill bit

Bead Key

A
B
C
D
E

Key-plates come in a variety of shapes and sizes, so tailor the instructions to fit the piece you are working with.

Copper Elbow Choker

T he copper pipe fitting section of the home improvement store caught my eye and reminded me of those copper-lined faceted beads I had been saving. Surely I could find something there to use with those beads—and I did! You can coat the copper pieces with a clear sealer to keep them bright or let them tarnish naturally as I did with this piece.

For the center:

1 Single-thread your needle with as much filament as you can handle.

2 String on enough dark copper-lined 8º seed beads to go around the middle of the copper elbow.

3 Pass the needle through the beads again and secure the thread, but leave it attached.

4 Referring to the instructions in for basic Peyote stitch, pages 22 and 23, begin weaving your first row of Peyote on the inside curve of the elbow. You will end up with one row on either side of the center ring.

5 Count four beads from the center of the curve and begin making what is actually the third row on one side. End it four beads short of the middle on the other side. You want to have an eight-bead strip two beads wide in the middle of the curve, as shown (Figure 5-11).

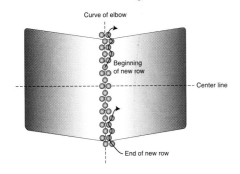

The strip in the middle is eight beads long and three beads wide counted on the diagonal.

Figure 5-11

6 Continue weaving rows on one side, dropping off a bead at either end until you are down to two beads (Figure 5-12).

Figure 5-12

7 Repeat steps 5 and 6 on the other side of center row and set woven copper elbow center piece aside.

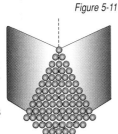

For the neck strap:

1 Cut five pieces of bead wire, each about 20" long.

2 Tie a waste bead on one end of one wire and alternate dark copper-lined 8º beads with the clear faceted beads until you have six 8º beads and five faceted beads and then finish the pattern sequence with a spacer bead, as shown in Figure 5-13. Repeat this pattern seven more times and then end the strand with an 8º bead.

Figure 5-13

3 Repeat step 2 for the other four wire pieces, but each time, start with one fewer bead in the first pattern and put the extra beads at the other end with the intent of offsetting the spacer beads so they don't all lay together.

4 When done stringing all five strands and after making sure they are the same lengths, pass the ends of all five strands through five 8º beads, two crimp beads, and around the clasp. Then pass wires back through the crimp beads and the five 8º beads.

5 Crimp the crimp beads tightly around the wires.

6 Cut the ends of the wires off about ½" into the beading.

7 Repeat steps 4 through 6 for the other end.

8 Hold one end of the necklace in either hand and twist the strands until they form a loose rope. Insert one end into the bead-woven elbow and work it to the center of the strand.

From hardware (at left) to hardly recognizable as something found at the hardware store.

Materials

- 45º ½" copper pipe elbow
- 200 copper-lined 6mm clear faceted beads
- 35 copper 3mm x 6mm fluted spacer beads
- 10 grams clear dark copper-lined 8º beads
- 4 large gold crimp beads
- Copper toggle clasp
- 49-strand bead-stringing wire
- White braided filament line
- 100" bead wire
- Size 10 sharps needle
- Crimp pliers
- Wire cutter

Fuses Bracelet

This bracelet is made with automotive fuses that are available in any store with an automotive department. This technique will work on all sorts of tubular objects. You can also make it longer and make a necklace.

1 Referring to the basic Peyote stitch instructions on pages 22 and 23, weave the purple links 13 beads long and four rows across using purple 14º seed beads, as shown in Figure 5-14. Do not join the ends together. Make five purple Peyote links and set aside.

Figure 5-14

2 Single-thread your needle with 1 yard of thread and tie a waste bead 4" from the end.

3 Thread on 18 turquoise 14º seed beads and pass the needle back through them to create a ring. Slip this ring over the glass part of one fuse and pull the ring of beads snugly.

4 Begin weaving around the fuse with Peyote stitch, in a pattern similar to that shown in Figure 5-15. Remove the waste bead, weave the thread end into the piece, and cut the end off.

Figure 5-15

5 When you have completed the 23 rows of the Peyote piece, use 18 turquoise 14º seed beads to make the straps from one side of the piece to the other on each end, as shown in Figure 5-16.

6 Repeat steps 2 through 5 three more times for a total of four bead-woven fuses.

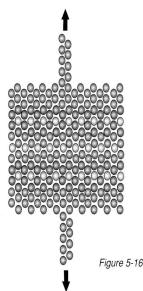

Figure 5-16

7 Place a purple Peyote link through the turquoise straps of two fuses and join the ends of the purple links. Continue to link the other fuses onto this "chain," ending both ends with purple links.

8 Take a new thread length through the center of the purple link on one of the ends of the bracelet and string on 15 purple 14º seed beads and the round silver bead.

9 String on three more purple seed beads and pass the needle back through the round silver bead and the 15 purple seed beads, as shown (Figure 5-17). Work the thread back through the beads several times and tie the end off.

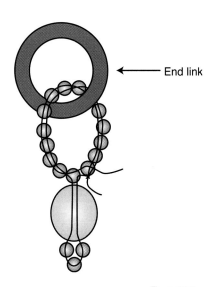

← End link

Figure 5-17

10 On the other end, attach a loop of approximately 33 purple seed beads to the purple Peyote link. Pass the thread through the loop several times to strengthen the piece and tie the end off.

Materials
- Several automotive fuses
- 2 grams turquoise 14º seed beads
- 2 grams purple 14º seed beads
- 1 gram clear silver-lined 14º seed beads
- 10mm round silver bead
- Brown Silamide thread
- Size 12 beading needle

The colorful beading around these automotive fuses creates a bracelet that no one can refuse!

Myrna Fligg used a heart-shaped tea infuser as the base for this necklace. She also makes beautiful Christmas ornaments with the larger infusers.

This Ladybug Springs Bracelet is a whimsical piece made with tiny silver springs and perfect for the young girl in your life. Notice how the tiny silver springs wouldn't stay on the bead wire without putting the size 8° beads on the line first.

A variation of the Ladybug Springs Bracelet (at right), this Teal Springs Bracelet combines teal flower beads and tiny silver springs for a more elegant effect.

ALL THAT GLITTERS MIGHT BE GLASS

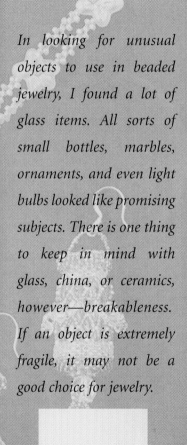

In looking for unusual objects to use in beaded jewelry, I found a lot of glass items. All sorts of small bottles, marbles, ornaments, and even light bulbs looked like promising subjects. There is one thing to keep in mind with glass, china, or ceramics, however—breakableness. If an object is extremely fragile, it may not be a good choice for jewelry.

Green Perfume Bottle Necklace

This bottle was a flea market find. The shape was just right to use a right-angle weave doughnut for the center.

For the beaded center:

1 Single-thread your needle with 2 yards of filament.

2 String on 15 gold 11º seed beads and tie them into a ring 6" from the end of the thread.

3 Hold the ring between the thumb and forefinger of your opposite hand and take the needle through the first bead next to the knot, string on five gold 11º seed beads, and pass back through the bead in the same direction. Pass through the next bead and pull the thread snugly, making a loop, as shown in Figure 6-1.

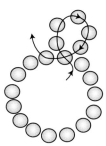

Figure 6-1

4 String on three gold beads and pass through the two side beads of the previous loop, as shown in Figure 6-2. Continue in this manner around the ring.

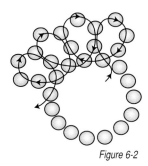

Figure 6-2

5 To make the last ring, you will pass through two right-most beads of the first loop made, thread on one gold bead, and pass down the two left-most beads of the second-to-last loop, as shown in Figure 6-3.

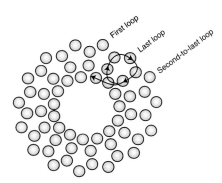

Figure 6-3

6 Bring the thread back through the first loop until it comes out the top point bead.

7 String on one green 8º seed bead and pass the needle through the top point bead of the next loop. Repeat this process around the looped area, as shown in Figure 6-4.

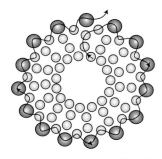

Figure 6-4

8 Pass around the ring a second time, adding in a gold 11º seed bead between each green 8º seed bead. The gold 11º seed beads added in this step should sit on the point beads of the first loops, as shown in Figure 6-5.

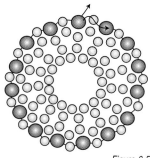

Figure 6-5

(continued)

Materials

- Round, flat, green perfume bottle
- 2 grams silver-lined green aurora borealis 8º seed beads
- 10 grams gold-plated 11º seed beads
- 4 gold 6mm round faceted beads
- 10mm green round faceted bead
- 15mm x 5mm gold dagger bead
- Gold toggle clasp
- 2 gold split rings
- 2 gold clamshell tips
- Gray braided filament line
- Size 10 beading needle

9 For the next row, bring the needle out the side of a green 8° seed bead, string on seven gold 11° seed beads, and pass back through the initial green bead in the same direction, making a loop. Continue through the gold bead on either side of the initial green bead and then through the next green bead. Pull snugly. Repeat this looping process, as shown in Figure 6-6, until you have gone all the way around the ring.

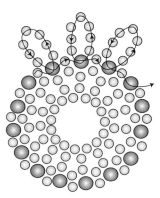

Figure 6-6

10 Pass around the ring again, adding one gold, one green, and another gold bead between each point bead of the loops of the previous row, as shown in Figure 6-7.

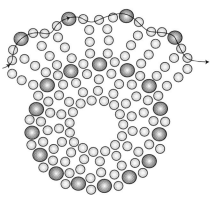

Figure 6-7

11 For the last row, come out of a green bead of the previous row and string on three gold, one green, and three more gold beads, passing back through the initial green bead to a make a loop. Continue through three gold beads next to the green of the previous row and through the next green bead. Pull snugly. Repeat this looping process, as shown in Figure 6-8, until you have gone all the way around the ring.

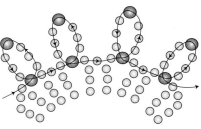

Figure 6-8

12 Place the needle on the tail of the thread in the center of the piece and string on one gold faceted bead. Take the thread directly across the ring, entering one of the gold seed beads of that ring and weaving the thread through the ring. Take the thread back through the center gold faceted bead again, work through the beading, tie thread off, and trim the end.

13 Repeat steps 1 through 12 to create another beaded medalion for the other side of the bottle.

For the bottle:

1 Cut 2 feet of thread, place a needle on each end, and then string on a green 8° seed bead and center it on the thread length.

2 Place the two beaded centers together, matching the outside loops. (This is the same concept as if you were to place wrong sides of circular fabric pieces together so they could be stitched together.)

3 Pass one needle through a green point bead on one beaded center and the other needle through the corresponding green point bead on the other beaded center. Then string a green bead on one needle and pass the second needle through it from the other direction, as shown in Figure 6-9. Pull snugly.

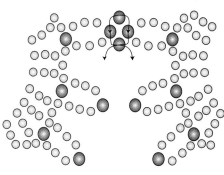

Figure 6-9

4 On each needle, string on one gold seed bead, one green seed bead, and another gold.

5 String a green seed bead on one needle and pass the second needle through it from the opposite direction. Pull snugly.

6 Pass each needle through the green point bead of the next loop, as in step 3, and repeat steps 3 through 6 around the beaded center pieces, creating the bead pattern as shown in Figure 6-10 around the rings. About halfway, insert the perfume bottle between the two beaded center pieces, and continue stitching them together. Tie off the threads.

For the neck straps:

1 Single-thread your needle with 4 feet of thread and place a needle on each end.

2 Pass one needle through one of the green seed beads you used in stitching the beaded centers around the perfume bottle and center this bead on the thread, just as though it were the first bead of the pattern in step 1 of the previous instructions.

3 Weave the threads through the side pattern for a few repeats to give it strength before starting the strap pattern.

4 Use Figure 6-10 as the bead pattern for the strap and repeat the pattern until you reach the desired length of approximately 12".

Figure 6-10

5 Finish the strap end with a clamshell bead tip, a crimp bead, and the clasp.

6 Repeat steps 1 through 6 for strap on other side.

For the dangle:

1 Single-thread your needle with 10" to 12" thread.

2 Pass the thread through the center bottom of the beaded bottle and string on three gold seed beads, one green seed bead, one gold faceted bead, one green faceted, one gold faceted, one green seed bead, three gold seed beads, one gold dagger, and three more gold seed beads.

3 Pass the thread back through the green seed bead, gold faceted bead, green faceted bead, gold faceted bead, and green seed bead.

4 String on three gold seed beads, pass the thread back into the bottom of the piece, and tie off the thread.

5 Optional: Make a loop of beads through the bottle cap if your bottle has a hole in the cap, as this one does.

Perfume bottles come in various shapes and sizes, so be sure to adapt the center beading pattern to match and you will create a one-of-a-kind necklace.

Chinese Pottery Necklace

The object that became the pendant part of this necklace was sold in a booth with blue-and-white Chinese pottery. It has a small hole at the top and a larger one at the bottom. No one seems to know what it is or what it is really used for, but it sure looked like a bead to me!

For the fringe:

1 Cut the head off the head pin and wrap the pin tightly around a pencil as many times as you can to make a large split ring. Set aside.

2 Cut a 4-foot length of Nymo thread, single-thread your needle, and tie the end of the thread to the split ring you made in step 1. Glue the knot and trim the tail to ¼".

3 Referring to Figure 6-11, string on 28 red seed beads, one 6mm disk bead, the oval blue-and-white ceramic bead, one 6mm disk bead, and a red seed bead.

Figure 6-11

4 Bring the thread around the last seed bead and pass back through the remaining bead sequence to the split ring. Pull the thread securely and tie it off on the ring, but don't cut the thread.

5 Continuing on the same thread as in step 4 and referring to Figure 6-12, string on 20 red seed beads and four blue seed beads. Skip the last three blue seed beads and pass back through the rest of the beads in the sequence to the split ring. Tie.

6 Repeat step 5 19 more times for a total of 10 fringe strands on either side of the first dragon strand, 20 strands total. Tie off securely. Glue the knot and trim the end to ¼".

For the neck straps:

1 Cut 1 yard of braided filament line, place a needle on each end, and tie the center of the thread securely around the now-fringed split ring.

2 Pass both needles through one 6mm disk bead and both holes in the pottery piece, large one first.

3 String the 13mm disk bead and one blue faceted bead onto both needles.

4 Separate the two threads.

5 On one thread, string one blue seed bead, one white round bead, one red oval, one blue faceted, one fluted white, one blue faceted, one red oval, and one blue-and-white round ceramic bead. The bead sequence is B-C-E-D-F-D-E-C.

6 Repeat the pattern from the first red oval (E-D-F-D-E-C) until you have five total of the pattern.

7 Substitute a 4mm round white bead for the large ceramic bead in the sequence and repeat the new sequence of E-D-F-D-E-G twice.

8 End the strand with a clamshell bead tip and a crimp bead.

9 Repeat steps 5 through 8 for the other thread.

10 Attach the split rings onto the clamshell tips on each strand and attach the clasp to the split rings.

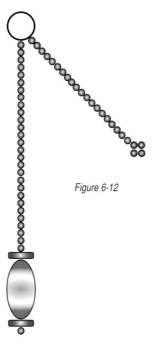

Figure 6-12

Materials

- Chinese pottery piece
- 5 grams red opaque 11° seed beads (A)
- 2 grams blue opaque 11° seed beads (B)
- 10 blue-and-white 14mm round ceramic beads (C)
- 25mm x 15mm blue-and-white oval ceramic bead (D)
- 29 cobalt blue 8mm faceted beads (E)
- 28 red 9mm x 5mm oval beads (F)
- 14 white 10mm fluted round beads (G)
- 6 white 6mm round beads (H)
- Red 13mm-diameter flat disk bead
- 3 red 6mm-diameter flat disk beads
- Silver toggle clasp
- 2 silver clamshell bead tips
- 2 silver split rings
- 2" silver head pin
- Nymo D white thread
- White braided filament line
- 2 size 10 beading needles
- Pencil
- Wire cutter

Bead Key

○ A
○ B
⬭ C
⬭ D
● E
⬭ F
○ G
○ H

Beach Glass Necklace

Beach glass can be found along many of our coastal beaches. The glass is naturally tumbled by the ocean, which gives it the soft, matte appearance. Be careful when choosing beach glass for jewelry. If it hasn't been in the water long enough, it can have sharp edges.

For the center piece:

1 Cut 2 yards of thread and place a needle on each end.

2 Thread a crimp bead on one needle and center it on the thread. Then pass both needles through a clamshell bead tip from the inside and close the clamshell around the crimp bead.

3 Choose a place on your glass piece where you can hold it securely with a band of right-angle weave and then referring to the instructions for this stitch on pages 18-20, use the pink 11° seed beads to make the band horizontally around the glass as tight as you can.

4 Join another band of pink 11° seed beads in right-angle weave to the first, but with this one going vertically and from front to back over the top of the glass piece. This second band also should be as tight as possible.

For the neck straps:

1 Cut a length of thread 2 yards long and single-thread your needle.

2 String on a crimp bead and a clamshell tip at the end.

3 With the pink seed beads, make five squares of right-angle weave and pass the thread through the outside hole of a flower bead.

4 Repeat step 3 eight more times, but alternate the two-petal edge of the flower bead with the three-petal edge for the outside hole as you go. Keep the aurora borealis sides of the flower beads facing the same direction, however.

5 After the ninth flower bead, complete three more right-angle weave squares, followed by a fourth square that picks up one pink seed bead in the band that crosses the top of the glass piece to complete the square. By using the bead from the vertical band to complete the final square on this side of the neck strand, the strand is seamlessly attached to the glass piece, as shown in Figure 6-13.

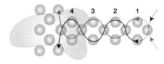

Figure 6-13

6 Work the thread through the vertical band to come out directly across from the pink seed bead used to complete the first strand, as shown in Figure 6-14. This bead then becomes the first in the four right-angle squares that begin the second strand. This time, however, you will complete it from the bottom up, so the sequence is reversed from that of step 5.

Figure 6-14

7 Repeat steps 1 through 4 for the inside strand of the neck strap, but instead of adding the flower beads, pass the thread through the open holes of the existing beads that are already attached to the outside strand.

8 After the ninth flower, complete three right-angle weave squares (not attached to the glass piece) and continue the inside strand pattern in reverse up the other side.

9 Attach the jump rings to the clamshell tips and then attach the rings to the clasp.

As you can see, no two pieces of beach glass are going to be exactly alike, so be sure to adapt your right-angle weave bands to fit around the piece you have to work with.

Materials
- Piece of clear beach glass
- 10 grams silver-lined pink 11° seed beads
- 18 light green aurora borealis 13mm x 11mm two-holed flower beads
- Gold two-strand clasp
- 4 gold clamshell tips
- 4 small crimp beads
- 4 gold jump rings
- White Nymo D thread
- Size 10 or 12 beading needle

Beaded Bottle Earrings

Small bottles can be used for all sorts of jewelry items. These are insulin vials.

For the center and top:

1 Referring to the vertical netting instructions on page 24 and using the dark rose and clear seed beads, complete a piece five sections wide. Use three rose beads for the sections and clear beads for the intersecting beads. Join the ends and place on the bottle.

2 Add a clear bead between each point bead around the neck of the bottle, as shown in Figure 6-15, and pull snugly.

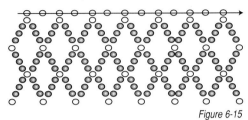

Figure 6-15

3 Referring to the Peyote stitch instructions on pages 22-23 and Figure 6-16, use clear seed beads to complete two rows of Peyote stitch around the neck of the bottle—more if needed for your bottle. Use rose beads for the final row.

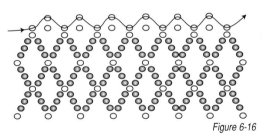

Figure 6-16

4 Bring the thread through one of the rose "up-beads," in the last row of the Peyote collar and string on three rose seed beads, one clear seed bead, and three more rose seed beads. Pass back through the initial rose up-bead in the same direction, thereby creating a beaded loop, as shown in Figure 6-17.

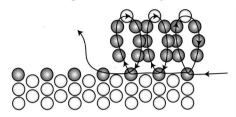

Figure 6-17

5 Repeat step 4 around the Peyote collar ring, making a loop off every rose up-bead.

6 Bring the thread through one clear point bead of one of the loops you just created, string on a clear seed bead, and continue on to the clear point bead of the next loop. Repeat for all the loops around the bottle top, pull the thread tightly, and make a half-hitch knot to secure, but do not cut the thread.

7 Thread on five rose seed beads and one clear seed bead and repeat the pattern three times. End with five more rose seed beads, slip the beaded thread through the earring finding, and take the thread back into the clear seed bead ring around the bottle top, directly across from where you first came up in step 6. Secure the thread and tie off the end.

8 Repeat steps 1 through 8 for the other bottle.

(continued)

Materials ▫▫▫▫▫▫▫▫▫▫▫▫▫▫▫▫▫▫▫

- ⭗ 2 small bottles (32.5mm tall with 15mm diameter)

- ⭗ 5 grams silver-lined clear 14º seed beads

- ⭗ 5 grams silver-lined dark rose 14º seed beads

- ⭗ 18 clear 4mm bicone crystals

- ⭗ 2 clear 8mm round faceted crystals

- ⭗ Silver earring findings

- ⭗ White Nymo B thread

- ⭗ Size 12 beading needle

For the bottom:

1 On the bottom of the vertical netting center section, bring the thread through one clear point bead, string on three clear seed beads, and then pass through the next clear point bead. Continue in this manner, adding three clear seed beads between each point bead around the bottom of the netted section.

2 Using clear seed beads, complete five rows of Peyote stitch with the clear beads of step 1 serving as the first two rows.

3 Continue with five more rows of Peyote stitch, but this time with the dark rose seed beads. This should take you to the bottom edge of the bottle, but if you are not to the edge, add an additional row or more of Peyote until you reach the bottom.

4 Bring the thread out of one of the up-beads in the last Peyote stitch row and string on two rose seed beads, one clear seed bead, two more rose seed beads, and one large crystal bead, as shown in Figure 6-18.

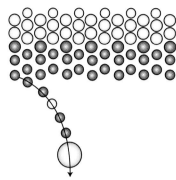

Figure 6-18

5 Next, string on five rose seed beads and one clear seed bead and repeat the bead sequence four times.

6 After the fourth clear seed bead of step 5, string on five more rose seed beads, one bicone crystal, and five more seed beads.

7 Follow with four repeats of one clear seed bead and five rose seed beads, making your way back up to the large round crystal bead, creating a looped fringe in the process.

8 Pass back up through the crystal and string on two rose seed beads, one clear seed bead, and two more rose seed beads.

9 Skip one up-bead to the right of the first one you came out of in step 4 and pass the thread through the Peyote work until you come to the third up-bead over.

10 Repeat steps 4 through 9 three more times, for a total of four looped fringes.

11 Repeat steps 1 through 10 for the other bottle.

Rather than discarding these tiny bottles, recycle them yourself in an innovative and interesting way.

SOMETHING'S FISHY

Chapter 7

My husband is an avid fisherman, so we go to sporting goods stores fairly often. Usually, these stores don't hold a lot of appeal for me, but after starting this project, I am now looking at fishing tackle in a completely different way. I have found many parts and pieces for use in jewelry. There are a lot of metal parts— like swivels and spinners— and they come in a variety of colors.

Spinners and Eye Pins Set

At larger sporting goods stores, you can purchase assorted boxes of spinner blades for making or repairing lures. The 30mm x 22mm spinner blades in this project came in a package of four colors, with 10 of each color. They were just crying out to be made into jewelry.

For the necklace:

1 Attach split rings to the holes in all the spinner blades.

2 On each 3" eye pin, thread on beads in the sequences shown in Figures 7-1 (A-B-CS-A-A-B-SS-A-A-B-GS-A-A-B-BS-A); 7-2 (A-B-SS-A-A-B-GS-A-A-B-BS-A-A-B-CS-A); and 7-3 (A-B-GS-A-A-B-BS-A-A-B-CS-A-A-B-SS-A).

Figure 7-1 (top pin)

Figure 7-2 (middle pin)

Figure 7-3 (bottom pin)

3 Referring to the sequence of illustrations in Figure 7-4 for assistance, if necessary, cut each pin to ⅜" past the end of the beads and turn a loop in the end of each, making sure the loops on both ends line up.

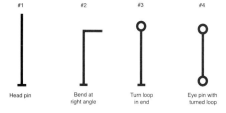

#1	#2	#3	#4
Head pin	Bend at right angle	Turn loop in end	Eye pin with turned loop

Figure 7-4

4 On each of the 1½" eye pins, thread on four black bicones, trim the pin to ⅜", and make an end loop.

5 Referring to the photo, use jump rings to attach a short beaded pin to each end of the 3" beaded eye pin you have designated for the bottom.

Step 5

6 Use jump rings to attach the second 3" beaded eye pin to the other end of the beaded short pins, as shown at right.

Step 6

7 Use jump rings to attach the remaining beaded short pins to each end of the second 3" beaded eye pin.

8 Use jump rings to attach each end of the last 3" beaded eye pin to the second set of beaded short pins, as shown. Be sure the curve of all the spinner blades points the same direction.

Step 8

9 Remove the center link from the chain, taking care to ensure you have the same number of links on each side. If the link numbers are not equal on both sides of the clasp, remove another link.

10 Attach the ends of the chain to each end of the top of the eye pin pendant.

For the earrings:

1 On one head pin, thread on a black bicone followed by a bugle, repeat once, and end with a bicone. The bead sequence is A-B-A-B-A.

2 Trim the pin and make a loop.

3 Bend the pin over your thumb gently to make a slight curve to match that of the spinner blade.

4 Attach the pins to the spinner blade with a split ring.

5 Attach the split ring to the earring finding.

6 Repeat steps 1 through 5 for the other earring.

Materials

- 30mm x 22mm spinner blades in the following colors:
  - 5 gold (GS)
  - 3 silver (SS)
  - 3 copper (CS)
  - 3 black (BS)
- 20" gold chain necklace
- 40 black 5mm faceted bicone beads (A)
- 16 black #1 bugle beads (B)
- 3 gold 3" eye pins
- 4 gold 1½" eye pins
- 2 gold 1½" head pins
- 16 gold jump rings
- 14 gold split rings
- Gold earring findings
- Wire cutter

Bead Key

△	GS
△	SS
△	CS
△	BS
◇	A
▭	B

91

From tackle to terrific!

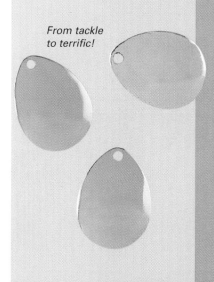

Fish Worm Necklace and Earrings Set

In one sporting goods store, I was mesmerized by a display of bins holding colorful rubber worms. I thought to myself, "Surely, I can use these bright objects in jewelry somehow." Choosing just the right ones was difficult when I didn't really know if my idea would work, but I purchased several anyway and decided that if my project didn't work, I could always use them for fish bait!

For the necklace:

1 Cut the worms with a sharp knife on a cutting board so you have three pieces 1⅜" long and two pieces ¾" long. Set aside.

Step 1

2 Use pliers to "cut" the memory wire to the 18½" length. Because memory wire will damage your wire cutter, hold the pliers at the point you wish to cut the wire and bend it back and forth in the same place until the wire snaps.

3 Turn a tiny loop in one end of the memory wire.

4 Thread on one black 6° seed bead, followed by a 10mm teal bead, and repeat this bead sequence 11 more times and then thread on a black spacer bead.

5 Carefully insert the beaded wire through the center of one of the 1⅜" rubber worm pieces. If you don't get it quite right, try it again on the same piece.

6 Thread on one spacer bead, one teal bead, and another spacer.

7 Add another of the 1⅜" worm pieces, followed by one spacer bead, one teal bead, and another spacer bead.

8 Add on the final 1⅜" worm piece, followed by one spacer.

9 Thread on one teal, followed by one black 6° seed bead, and repeat this bead sequence 11 more times.

10 Make a tiny loop in the other end of the wire.

For the earrings:

1 Thread one black 8° seed bead, one black 6° seed bead, and one spacer bead onto one head pin.

2 Insert the beaded pin through the center of one ¾" worm piece.

3 Thread on one spacer bead, one teal bead, and one black 8° seed bead.

4 Trim the pin to ⅜" and make a loop. Refer to Figure 7-4, page 91, for assistance with this step, if necessary.

5 Attach earring finding to the loop with a jump ring.

6 Repeat steps 1 through 5 for the other earring.

Materials

- 18½" piece memory wire
- 3 chartreuse knobby fish worms
- 10 black 8mm spacer beads
- 26 black 6° seed beads
- 4 black 8° seed beads
- 28 translucent teal 10mm fluted round beads
- 2 silver 2" head pins
- Silver earring findings
- 2 silver jump rings
- Cutting board
- Sharp knife
- Pliers

Tip

Before starting your project, wash the worms with warm soapy water. Lay them on a towel and let them dry thoroughly. The worms have an oily coating on them that is not pleasant to work with and might stain clothing.

93

These fishing worms convert easily to jewelry that is sure to make you a great catch!

Swivels Jewelry Set

The chain links in this necklace and bracelet are brass swivels.

A swivel is used on a fishing reel to keep the line from twisting.

They work the same in a necklace.

For the necklace:

1 On a 2" eye pin, thread on beads in the sequence shown in Figure 7-5 (B-D-A-D-B), making sure to go through the two-petal side of the flower bead (A). Repeat this same bead sequence on four more 2" eye pins.

Figure 7-5

2 Trim all five beaded 2" eye pins to ⅜" and make a loop at the end of each. Set aside.

3 On a 2" eye pin, thread beads in the sequence shown in Figure 7-6 (E-C-E-C-E-A-E-C-E-C-E), again making sure to go through the two-petal side of the A-bead. Repeat this same bead sequence on three more 2" eye pins.

Figure 7-6

4 Trim all four beaded 2" eye pins from step 3 to ⅜" and make a loop at the end of each. Refer to Figure 7-4, page 91, for assistance with this step, if necessary. Set aside.

5 Begin necklace strand with a swivel and use a jump ring to attach it to one of the step 1 beaded pins.

6 Use a jump ring to attach another swivel to the step 1 pin and then use a jump ring to attach the swivel to a beaded pin from step 2.

7 Continue alternating pins with swivels, as in steps 5 and 6, until you get all the pins attached.

8 End the neck stand with a swivel.

9 Use jump rings to attach clasps to each end of the neck strand.

For the bracelet:

1 Thread three pins the same as step 1 of the necklace instructions, making sure to go through the two-petal side of the flower bead.

2 Trim all three beaded 2" eye pins to ⅜" and make a loop at the end of each. Refer to Figure 7-4, page 91, for assistance with this step, if necessary. Set aside.

3 Referring to Figure 7-7, thread one 2" eye pin with one gold disk, one teal druk, one gold disk, one teal druk, and one gold disk. Then thread onto the three-petal side of the flower beads already attached to a step 1 pin. Finish bead sequence with one gold disk, one teal druk, one gold disk, one teal druk, and one gold disk. Repeat this step two more times.

Figure 7-7

4 Trim all three beaded 2" eye pins from step 3 to ⅜" and make a loop at the end of each. Refer to Figure 7-4, page 91, for assistance with this step, if necessary. Set aside.

5 Bend the beaded pin pairs in a slight curve to fit your wrist and use jump rings to attach each beaded pin pair to the next.

6 Use jump rings to attach the swivels to a beaded pin pair at each end of the strand.

7 Use jump rings to join the swivels together.

8 Attach each end jump ring to the clasp with one or more jump rings to fit your wrist.

Materials

- ⊸ 16 brass ¾" swivels
- ⊸ 15 gold 2" eye pins
- ⊸ 2 gold 1" head pins
- ⊸ 12 teal aurora borealis 13mm x 11mm two-holed flower beads (A)
- ⊸ 18 teal aurora borealis 9mm x 6mm teardrop beads (B)
- ⊸ 28 teal aurora borealis 4mm druks (round beads) (C)
- ⊸ 18 gold 4mm metal round fluted beads (D)
- ⊸ 42 gold 4mm-diameter disk beads (E)
- ⊸ 2 gold clasps
- ⊸ Gold earring findings
- ⊸ 26 gold jump rings

Bead Key

A
B
C
D
E

For the earrings:

1 On one head pin, thread one teardrop bead and one gold fluted bead.

2 Trim the end and make a loop. Refer to Figure 7-4, page 91, for assistance with this step, if necessary.

3 Use a jump ring to attach the beaded pin to a swivel.

4 Use a jump ring to attach other end of the swivel to an earring finding.

5 Repeat steps 1 through 4 for the other earring.

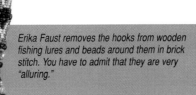

Erika Faust removes the hooks from wooden fishing lures and beads around them in brick stitch. You have to admit that they are very "alluring."

When you can't make up your mind which box of spinner blades to buy—get them both. You will probably find a way to use them. See how the smaller spinners can create pieces just as attractive as the larger ones did in the Spinners and Eye Pins Set from page 90. Who could tell you're wearing fishing tackle when it looks as stunning as this jewelry set?

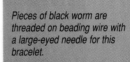

Pieces of black worm are threaded on beading wire with a large-eyed needle for this bracelet.

Copper and black beads, coupled with copper worms, are threaded onto bracelet memory wire to make this creation.

PLAYING GAMES WITH BEADING

Chapter 8

The Mahjongg tiles got me started on using game pieces as jewelry. I found the antique Bakelite dragon tiles at a show in Minneapolis, Minnesota. Since I collect dragons, I just couldn't pass them up. That led me to wondering what other game pieces I could turn into jewelry …

Dominoes Necklace and Earrings Set

Regular dominoes are rather big and heavy for a necklace. Not so with these small bone ones that I found at a gem show. I asked the vendor if they were real dominoes, and he assured me they were. They make a nice necklace and they aren't heavy to wear.

1 Drill a hole through one narrow end of each domino, as shown in Figure 8-1.

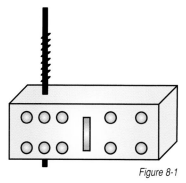

Figure 8-1

2 Double-thread your needle with 40" of thread. Securely tie a small crimp bead on the very end of the thread, glue the knot, trim the ends, and string on a clamshell tip.

3 String on beads in the sequence shown in Figure 8-2 (E-C-E-C-E-C-E-D-B-D). Repeat this sequence three more times.

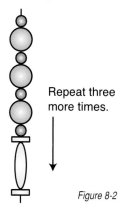

Repeat three more times.

Figure 8-2

4 String on beads, as well as the domino, in the sequence illustrated in Figure 8-3 (E-C-E-C-E-C-E-D-domino-D).

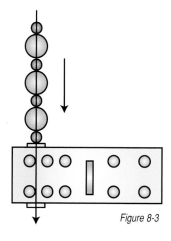

Figure 8-3

5 String on beads as shown in the sequence illustration in Figure 8-4 (E-D-A-D-E-D-C-D-E).

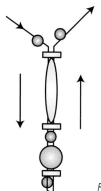

Figure 8-4

6 Bring the thread around the last green seed bead and pass back through the beads to the top disk spacer, skipping the first green seed bead. String on another green seed bead. You will now have a dangle with a green seed bead on either side (Figure 8-4).

7 String on one disk spacer bead, one domino, and another disk spacer bead.

8 Repeat steps 5 and 6 until you have a total of five dominoes strung and four bone dangles.

9 Finish the second half of the neck strap in the reverse order of steps 3 and 4.

10 End the strand as you began, with a clamshell bead tip and a crimp bead.

11 Use split rings on each strand end to attach the clamshell tips to the clasp.

For the earrings:

1 On the head pin, thread the following bead sequence: E-D-C-D-E-D-B-D-E.

2 Trim pin to ⅜" and make a loop. Refer to Figure 7-4, page 91, for assistance with this step, if necessary.

3 Use a split ring to attach the beaded pin to an earring finding.

4 Repeat steps 1 through 3 for the other earring.

Materials

- 5 bone 32mm x 12mm dominoes
- 4 bone 25mm pipe beads (A)
- 10 bone 12mm pipe beads (B)
- 36 agate 8mm beads (C)
- 54 gold 4mm disk spacer beads (D)
- 1 gram silver-lined green 11° seed beads (E)
- Gold toggle clasp
- 2 gold clamshell bead tips
- Gold earring findings
- 2 gold 2" head pins
- 4 gold split rings
- 2 small crimp beads
- Fine gray braided filament line
- Drill and ¹⁄₆₄" drill bit
- Size 10 beading needle

Bead Key

A

B

C

D

E

99

Scrabble Tiles Bracelet

This name bracelet is comprised of Scrabble tiles. These tiles are made of very fine-grained hard wood. Use a hand drill to make the holes, thereby cutting down on the possibility of breaking off the tile corners.

1. Drill holes approximately ⅛" from the edges of the wooden tile corners. Each tile will have four holes (one in each corner). Lay out the tiles in order to spell a name or another short word.

2. Cut 24" of thread and place a needle on each end.

3. Tie a crimp bead in the middle of the thread length, pass both needles through a clamshell bead tip, and close the clamshell around the crimp bead. Refer to Option 4 on page 16 for illustrated assistance, if necessary.

4. Pass both needles through three red 8° seed beads (more if your bracelet has fewer than six tiles) and then separate the needles.

5. String seven red 11° seed beads on each needle.

6. From the underside of tile, pass the top needle through the top corner hole and the bottom needle through the bottom corner hole in the same manner.

7. Thread approximately nine red 11° seed beads on each needle to go straight across the tile and put each needle through the opposite corner top and bottom tile holes.

8. String three red 11° seed beads on each needle.

9. Repeat steps 6 through 8 on the next tile.

10. Continue to repeat steps 6 through 8 across the bracelet.

11. When you come out the bottom of the corner holes of the last tile, string seven red 11° seed beads on each needle and pass both needles through three red 8° seed beads.

12. End the strand with a clamshell bead tip and a crimp bead, just as you began.

13. Use split rings to attach the clasp to the clamshell tips.

Materials ∘∘∘∘∘∘∘∘∘∘∘∘∘∘∘∘∘∘∘∘∘

- ➤ Scrabble tiles
- ➤ 2 grams red aurora borealis 11° seed beads
- ➤ 6 red aurora borealis 8° seed beads
- ➤ Gold clasp
- ➤ 2 gold clamshell tips
- ➤ 2 gold split rings
- ➤ 2 small crimp beads
- ➤ Gray braided filament line
- ➤ Size 10 beading needle
- ➤ Drill and ¼₄" drill bit

101

It's amazing that these wooden letter tiles can be used for more than just playing a board game on rainy days.

Mahjongg Tile Necklace

Drilling a hole sideways through this green dragon Mahjongg tile turned it into a bead. The green cloisonnè beads have been in my bead inventory for quite a while, as have the antique gold beads. This necklace seemed the right project to use them on.

1 Double-thread your needle with 24" of thread.

2 Tie a crimp bead on the end, glue the knot, string on a clamshell tip, and close it around the crimp bead.

3 String on beads in the sequence that is shown in Figure 8-5 (E-E-E-C-D-C-E-C-D-C).

4 Follow with beads in the sequence shown in Figure 8-6 (E-C-D-C-E-A). Repeat this pattern twice more.

5 Repeat the pattern again, but exchange the 10mm cloisonné bead with a 12mm cloisonné bead (E-C-D-C-E-B), as shown in Figure 8-7.

6 Repeat the step 4 bead sequence (E-C-D-C-E-A).

7 String on one gold round bead, the tile, and one gold round bead.

8 Follow with the reverse of the step 4 bead sequence, which is A-E-C-D-C-E.

9 Thread on the reverse of step 5, which is B-E-C-D-C-E.

10 Repeat the step 8 bead sequence (A-E-C-D-C-E) three times.

11 Follow with the reverse of the step 3 bead sequence, which is C-D-C-E-C-D-C-E-E-E.

12 Thread on a clamshell tip and a crimp bead and tie off the threads against the crimp bead. Glue the knot, trim the ends, and close the clamshell bead tip.

13 Use split rings to attach the clasp to the clamshell tips.

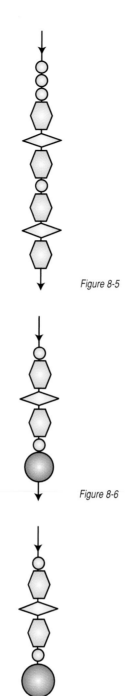

Figure 8-5

Figure 8-6

Figure 8-7

Materials □□□□□□□□□□□□□□□□□□□□□
- ○- Mahjongg tile
- ○- 8 green cloisonné 10mm round beads (A)
- ○- 2 green cloisonné 12mm round beads (B)
- ○- 28 gold-plated 6mm eight-sided beads (C)
- ○- 14 yellow matte 5mm x 6mm fluted beads (D)
- ○- 30 gold 2.5mm round metal beads (E)
- ○- Gold toggle clasp
- ○- 2 gold clamshell bead tips
- ○- 2 gold split rings
- ○- 2 small crimp beads
- ○- Gray braided filament line
- ○- Size 10 beading needle

Bead Key □□□□□□□□□□□□□□□□□□□□□

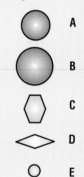

A

B

C

D

E

103

Mahjongg Tile Brooch

Mahjongg is a game that originated in China. It is usually played by four people with tiles that resemble dominoes. This dragon tile is made of Bakelite, an early plastic made from formaldehyde and phenol. Bakelite objects are highly collectible.

For brooch center:

1 With gem glue, adhere the tile to the center of one piece of leather and allow the glue to dry thoroughly before continuing.

2 Referring to the instructions for a ladder stitch with bugle and seed beads, page 21, use bronze bugle beads and red 11° seed beads to make a ladder, as shown in Figure 8-8, long enough to go around the edges of the Mahjongg tile. Join the ends to form a ring that will fit very snugly around the tile. Tie off the threads and place the ring around the tile.

Figure 8-8

3 Single-thread your needle with a new thread 1 yard long. Tie a sloppy knot in the thread end and bring the needle up from the underside of the leather and through one set of beads in the ladder. Pull the thread up tightly so the knot is against the leather.

4 String on one bronze 11° seed bead and take the thread down through the bugle-seed bead ladder "rung" and back through the leather.

5 Bring the needle back up through the leather, pass through the next "rung" of beads in the ladder (as in step 3), and repeat step 4. Continue in this manner all the way around the ladder.

6 For extra security in keeping the tile in place, bring the thread up four bronze seed beads away from a corner and thread on seven red 11° seed beads to cross the corner diagonally. Pass the needle back through the diagonal bead "rung" that is four bronze seed beads from the corner and down into the leather.

7 Bring the needle up through a bead "rung" four beads away from the next corner and repeat step 6.

8 Repeat steps 6 and 7 twice more for the remaining corners.

9 Come up from the underside with a new thread and string on enough red 8° seed beads to make a ring large enough to encircle the tile and ladder.

10 Referring to the couching instructions on page 26, couch the ring of seed beads from step 9 in place next to the ladder.

11 Trim the leather close to the line of beads, without cutting the threads. Use the beaded piece as a pattern and trim the extra piece of red leather to the same size. Set the extra piece of leather aside.

For the fringe:

1 Rethread your needle, tie a large knot on the thread end, and bring the needle up through leather from underneath, coming out between the ladder and the red seed bead ring towards the top of the piece, as shown in Figure 8-9.

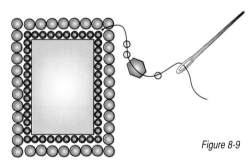

Figure 8-9

2 String on two bronze 11° seed beads, a larger red bead from your assortment, and another bronze 11° seed bead.

3 Bring the thread around and pass back through the large red bead, two bronze seed beads, and down through the leather.

4 Bring the needle back up through leather close to the first fringe you made in steps 1 through 3.

(continued)

Materials

- Mahjongg tile
- 48 bronze 9mm (#3) bugle beads (A)
- 100 red 11° seed beads (B)
- 200 bronze 11° seed beads (C)
- 60 red 8° seed beads (D)
- 100 assorted red beads (E)
- 2 pieces 2" x 2½" red leather
- 1" pin back
- Red or dark gray Nymo D thread
- #10 sharps needle
- Gem glue
- Fabric glue
- Scissors

5 Repeat steps 2 through 4 for the second fringe and continue around the piece in this manner. Vary the beads and the fringe lengths. Make the fringe dangles longer at the bottom and shorter on the sides and top. You can use more than one larger bead per dangle. Be inventive.

6 When the fringe is complete around the entire piece, bring the needle down through the leather, tie off the thread, and cut the end.

For the back:

1 Mark the placement for the pin back on the inside of the second piece of leather about ½" down from the top of the piece.

2 Make small cuts where the ends of the pin backing plate should be, as shown in Figure 8-10.

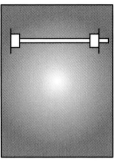

Figure 8-10

3 Slip the ends of the pin through the cuts in the leather from the inside out.

4 Use fabric glue to attach the pin-backed leather piece to the back of the brooch.

Mahjongg tiles come in a variety of designs, so pick your colors and detailing to match.

BUTTONS AND COINS

Chapter 9

Buttons are jewelry for clothing. Even though their main purpose is functional, they can be a beautiful adornment. They are often made of—or set with—semiprecious stones, rhinestones, precious metals, or shells. They can be made out of the same materials as beads and can be just as attractive. They can be used in jewelry in a number of ways.

Coins also fit into this category. Many coins have lovely designs. And because they are usually flat, they can be cabochon set, have holes drilled into them, or can be beaded around.

Pearl-and-Gold Button Necklace

A button chain is not a new concept. This one, however, is different because of the gold seed beads serpentined through the buttons.

For the main strand:

1 Double-thread your needle so you have about 40" of thread.

2 Tie a crimp bead on the thread end, leaving about a 4" tail. Pass through a clamshell tip from the inside and push down the thread until it covers the crimp bead, but do not close the clamshell.

3 Thread on four gold 11° seed beads and pass the needle through a hole of one button from the back to the front.

4 String on one gold 11° seed bead, one 8° seed bead, and another gold 11° seed bead. Pass through the hole directly opposite the one you came up through, as shown in Figure 9-1, and pull the thread all the way through until the beads are snug against the button.

Figure 9-1

5 String on next button, going through one hole from the front, across the backside, and back up through the hole directly opposite the one you came down through initially. Pull the thread through so buttons rest flat on one another, offset about one-half button, as shown in Figure 9-2.

Figure 9-2

6 String on the next button from the backside and pull the thread up snugly.

7 Referring to Figure 9-3, repeat steps 3 through 5 once more.

Figure 9-3

8 Continue to repeat steps 3 through 6 until necklace is the desired length. You will be creating two rows of buttons for the completed strand: one on top of the other and offset by a half-button. The sample is 21" long.

9 Finish the strand by adding four gold 11° seed beads, the clamshell tip, and the crimp bead. Trim the thread end to 4".

For the strand embellishment:

1 Double-thread your needle with 40" of thread and tie the end of the thread to one of the crimp beads already in the clamshell tips, leaving a 4" tail.

2 Pass the needle through a clamshell tip and the first four gold 11° seed beads on the main strand.

3 String on five gold 11° seed beads and pass the needle through one of the side holes in the first bottom button of the main strand, as shown in Figure 9-4, and come out the front.

Figure 9-4

4 String on 11 gold 11° seed beads, curve around the second top button on the main strand, and take the needle down through the side hole of the next bottom button, as shown in Figure 9-5 for the front view and Figure 9-6 for the back view.

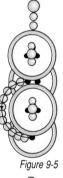

Figure 9-5

5 Pass the needle up through hole directly opposite that which you came down through in the previous step.

Figure 9-6

6 String on 11 gold 11° seed beads, curve around the opposite side of the next top button, and take the needle down in the side hole of the next bottom button. The eleven seed beads will alternate from side to side as you progress down the strand, as shown in Figure 9-7.

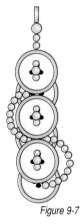

Figure 9-7

7 Repeat steps 5 and 6 to the other end of the strand.

8 To finish the strand, string on five gold 11° seed beads and pass the needle through four existing gold 11° seed beads, a clamshell tip, and a crimp bead.

9 Tie off all the threads against the crimp beads, glue the knots, trim the ends, and close the clamshell tips.

10 Use split rings to attach the clasp to both ends.

Materials

- 81 pearl-and-gold ½" four-hole buttons
- 529 gold metallic 11° seed beads
- 41 gold metallic 8° seed beads
- Gold 14mm round one-strand clasp
- 2 gold clamshell bead tips
- 2 gold 5mm split rings
- 2 small crimp beads
- White Nymo D bead thread
- Size 10 beading needle

Old Button Necklace

This button has been in my home for a very long time.
In order to use it like a beaded cabochon, I had to figure out
what to do with the molded metal shank. Cutting it off wasn't
a good option, so instead, I cut several pieces of leather, made
holes in the middle, and stacked them up behind the button.
Then, I beaded around the button just as with any cabochon.

For the beaded center:

1 Back the button with leather glued to it if necessary to hide the shank. Trim the leather close to the button edge. Glue it to one larger piece of leather and allow it to dry thoroughly.

2 Referring to the instructions on pages 25 and 26 for making a beaded collar, use black 11º seed beads for four rows (or as many as necessary) and then use bronze 11º seed beads for the second-to-last row. Go back to the black 11º seed beads for the final row.

3 Make a ring of black 4mm round beads long enough to go around the base of the collar. Pass through the beads again to strengthen the ring and couch the ring into place, referring to the couching instructions on page 26, if necessary.

4 The next row out is made up of a ring of bronze 11º seed beads alternating with black 4mm faceted beads. Couch the ring in place.

5 The outside row is a ring of black 8º seed beads alternating with black teardrop beads. Couch it in place.

6 Trim the leather, being careful not to cut any threads. Use the beaded piece as a pattern to cut the backing piece of leather. Do not attach the backing at this point.

For the fringe:

1 For the center fringe, refer to Figure 9-8 and string on one bronze 11º seed bead and one black 8º seed bead and repeat this pattern (B-D) six more times.

2 Still referring to Figure 9-8, string on beads in the following sequence: F-G-C-G-C-G-F-B-A-B-H-B-A-B.

3 Bring the thread around to form a loop and re-enter the bead string at the black 4mm faceted bead that is the eighth-from-the-last strung and continue back through the strand to the top. Secure the thread.

4 Move to the side and start the next fringe. Each fringe decreases two seed beads as you move away from the center. The outside two fringe strands have six seed beads at the top, as shown in Figure 9-9.

For the neck straps:

1 Referring to the scalloped Peyote instructions on page 29, make a neck strap long enough to go over your head (approximately 27").

2 Sew each strap end to the top of the beaded button pendant.

3 Glue or sew the leather in place on the back of the piece.

Figure 9-8

Figure 9-9

Materials

- Old button
- 20 grams black 11º seed beads (A)
- 10 grams bronze 11º seed beads (B)
- 18 bronze 8º seed beads (C)
- 68 black 8º seed beads (D)
- 23 black 4mm round beads (E)
- 39 black 4mm round faceted beads (F)
- 27 black 6mm round faceted beads (G)
- 44 black 6mm x 4mm teardrop beads (H)
- 2 2½" squares black leather
- Craft and gem glue
- Black Nymo B or D thread
- Size 10 sharps needle

Bead Key

- ● A
- ○ B
- ○ C
- ● D
- ⬡ F
- ⬡ G
- ⬟ H

111

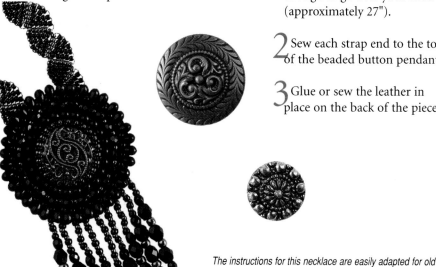

The instructions for this necklace are easily adapted for old buttons of different sizes and designs. For example, use smaller beads on the beaded collar for smaller buttons or fewer rows and/or smaller beads in the collar for a button of a similar size where you would like more of the center design to show.

Chinese Coin
Necklace and Earrings Set

T his reproduction of an old Chinese coin appealed to me because it has dragons around the center of the piece. The side shown has Chinese characters around the hole.

For the dangle::

1 Drill a hole in bottom of the coin, close to the outer edge.

2 On a 2½" head pin, thread on beads in the following sequence: E-H-G-D-E-A-E.

3 Trim the head pin and make a loop. Refer to Figure 7-4, page 91, for assistance with this step, if necessary.

4 Use a jump ring to attach the dangle to the coin through the drilled hole.

For the neck straps:

1 Single-thread your needle with 30" of thread and tie a crimp bead on the end, leaving a 4" tail. String on a clamshell tip from the inside.

2 String on beads in the sequence shown in Figure 9-10 (E-D-C-D). Repeat this sequence four more times.

Figure 9-10

3 Repeat the step 2 sequence, but use a bronze 8mm faceted bead in place of the 6mm faceted bead (E-D-B-D), as shown in Figure 9-11.

Figure 9-11

4 Repeat the step 2 sequence (E-D-C-D) once again.

5 String on one rose seed bead and one black tube bead.

6 Repeat the step 2 sequence (E-D-C-D).

7 Repeat steps 5 and 6.

8 Repeat the step 3 bead sequence (E-D-B-D).

9 Repeat the step 2 sequence (E-D-C-D) once again.

10 Repeat steps 5 and 6.

11 String on bead sequence E-A-E-D followed by enough bronze 11° seed beads (F) for a strand long enough to go through the hole in the coin and back around plus three more.

12 Pass the needle back through the three seed beads closest to the last bronze rondelle and continue back through all the beads in the strand.

13 Pull the thread tight and pass through clamshell tip. Tie off the threads against the crimp bead, glue the knot, trim the thread, and close the clamshell.

14 Repeat steps 1 through 13 for the second neck strap.

15 Use jump rings to attach the clamshell tips to the clasp.

For the earrings:

1 On a head pin, thread on beads in the sequence shown in Figure 9-12 (E-D-H-E-I-E).

Figure 9-12

2 Trim the head pin to ⅜" and make a loop at the end above the beads. Refer to Figure 7-4, page 91, for assistance with this step, if necessary.

3 Attach the head pin to an earring finding.

4 Repeat steps 1 through 3 for the other earring.

Materials

- 40mm brass Chinese coin
- 9 black 18mm x 6mm tube beads (A)
- 4 bronze 8mm faceted round beads (B)
- 20 bronze 6mm faceted round beads (C)
- 53 bronze 3mm x 6mm fluted rondelles (D)
- 43 rose 8° seed beads (E)
- 1 gram bronze 11° seed beads (F)
- 8mm black round bead (G)
- 3 bronze 6mm x 6mm faceted teardrop beads (H)
- 2 black 6mm round beads (I)
- Gold toggle clasp
- 2 gold clamshell bead tips
- 2 small crimp beads
- 2½" gold head pin
- 2 gold 1½" head pins
- Earring findings
- 3 gold jump rings
- Gray braided filament line
- Size 10 beading needle
- Drill and 1/64" drill bit

Bead Key

A

B

C

D

E

H

I

These brass plates go on the cabinet or drawer before you put the knob on. Holes drilled around the center provided lots of places to put beads. Those packages of assorted beads you find at craft stores made these brooches "one-of-a-kind" pieces.

Meet Princess Sandra Mae who is all decked out in her stunning button dress. The princess was beaded by national instructor, Cheryl Erickson.

My beading buddies call this piece the Las Vegas Bracelet and asked to borrow it when they went gambling. I did this one in square stitch, but the pattern also could be done on a loom.

SHELLS AND OTHER NATURAL THINGS

Chapter 10

Unusual found objects are all around us, especially in nature. There are all sorts of seeds, shells, rocks, and plants that can be used in jewelry. Keep your eyes open on your next outdoors adventure.

Beaded Gourd Necklace

This little gourd measures about 3" long from bottom to the end of stem. Gourds like this are sold as "jewelry gourds" to be wood-burned, carved, and painted. I set about covering this one with beads. Four different weaving techniques were used in this little project. You will need to alter your beading pattern to fit the contours of the gourd you use, since all gourds are shaped differently.

For the center:

1 Referring to the vertical netting instructions on page 24 and using both the peach and aqua 11º seed beads, do a section of netting wide enough to go from the base of the stem to nearly the bottom of the gourd and long enough to go all the way around the bowl of the gourd. The aqua seed beads make up the majority of the design, with the peach beads used as intersection and point beads. Lace the ends together to form a tube. Place the netting on the gourd.

2 With a new length of thread, bring the needle through one of the peach point beads at the top of the netting, thread on another peach seed bead, if needed, and pass through the next point bead. Continue in this manner until you complete a ring. Pull the thread tightly to help the netting follow the gourd's curve more closely.

3 Work the thread through to the bottom of the vertical netting section and repeat step 2 for the bottom.

4 Bury a new thread in the work and string on an aqua 11º seed bead to begin a row of Peyote stitch at the top of the piece, referring to the basic instructions on pages 22 and 23, if necessary. Weave up the neck and stem of the gourd with approximately five rows of aqua seed beads, followed by four rows of peach, another 14 rows of aqua, and then approximately 18 rows of peach to the end. You may need to increase or decrease beads per row, depending on your gourd's dimensions. You also may need to adjust the number of rows necessary to cover the neck of the gourd.

For the tassel:

1 Count the beads in the bottom row created in step 3 of the previous instructions and divide the number of beads by the number of strands you want in your tassel. The sample shown here ended up with six strands.

2 Bury a new thread in the work and bring the needle out between two beads in the bottom row.

3 Referring to Figure 10-1, string on two peach seed beads, one aqua 8º seed bead, two peach seed beads, and another aqua 8º seed bead.

4 Add one peach seed bead and three aqua 11º seed beads. Repeat this same bead sequence six more times (Figure 10-1).

5 Thread one peach seed bead, one aqua 8º seed bead, and another peach seed bead (Figure 10-1). Bring the thread around the last peach bead and pass the needle back through all the beads to the top.

Gathering bead →

Figure 10-1

6 Pass the needle through the bottom ring to where you need to come out.

7 String on two peach seed beads, one aqua 8º seed bead, two peach seed beads, and then pass the needle through the center aqua 8º seed bead on the first strand you created. This aqua 8º is the gathering bead.

8 Repeat steps 4 through 7 until you are done with the number of tassels you desire.

9 Bury the thread end in the work.

For the neck strap:

1 Referring to the instructions for Potawatomi weave on page 30, alternate the peach and aqua 11º seed beads to weave a strap that is the desired length (sample is 36").

2 Place one strap end on the side of gourd, slightly below where the neck begins, and stitch it to the netting.

3 Repeat step 2 for the other side.

Materials ○○○○○○○○○○○○○○○○○○○

-○- Jewelry gourd

-○- 30 grams aqua luster 11º seed beads (A)

-○- 20 grams silver-lined dark peach 11º seed beads (B)

-○- 13 aqua 8º seed beads (C)

-○- White Nymo D beading thread

-○- Size 10 or 12 beading needle

Bead Key ○○○○○○○○○○○○○○○○○

O A

O B

O C

Tip

When determining the size of your vertical netting section in step 1, remember that you have to use an uneven number of sections to make vertical netting work. You can experiment using two, three, or four beads in each section to get it to work out for length. Even though vertical netting is an elastic weaving and it will conform to your gourd's shape, the beaded section still has to fit around the widest part.

Shell Brooch

These two pieces of shell just naturally seemed to go together.
The purple iris beads reflect the colors in the cabochon shell.

For the center:

1 Referring to the beaded collar instructions on pages 25 and 26, use the purple 11º seed beads to make the collar. Make the second-to-last row with bronze 14º beads and the last row with black 14º beads. Since the shell is fairly flat, the beaded bezel comes in over the top of it.

2 String a ring of purple 8º seed beads long enough to go around the collar and couch in place.

3 String a ring of bronze 11º seed beads long enough to go around the beaded bezel and couch that in place between the collar and the outside ring. It will sit just above the outside ring, as shown in Figure 10-2.

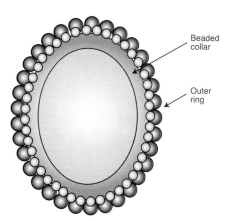

Beaded collar

Outer ring

Figure 10-2

4 Trim the leather close to the beads and use this piece as a template to cut a backing piece out of the other piece of leather. Set aside.

For the fringe:

1 Bring the needle out five beads from the bottom center and between the two purple 8º seed beads that made up the outside ring of the beaded center.

2 Thread on beads in the sequence shown in Figure 10-3 (A-A-A-F-C-C-C-F-C-G-C-H-B).

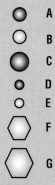

Figure 10-3

3 Bring the thread around the bottom bronze seed bead and pass back up through the strand, entering at the purple teardrop and continuing to the top.

4 Pass the needle through the next purple 8º seed bead of the ring where you began in step 1.

5 Repeat steps 2 through 4 nine more times, for a total of 10 bottom fringe strands.

6 Bring the thread out between two beads in the outer ring, and string on one purple 8º seed bead and one bronze 11º seed bead.

7 Bring the thread around the bottom bronze seed bead and pass the needle back through the purple 8º bead and back into the ring. Take needle through the next two beads in the outer ring (either direction will do) and come back out between those two beads, as shown in Figure 10-4.

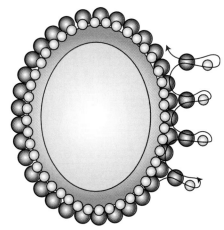

Figure 10-4

8 Repeat steps 6 and 7 around the ring. A new pair should rest between every two beads around the ring. You have made picots.

For the back:

1 Glue the backing to the beaded center piece.

2 When dry, glue the larger half-shell onto the leather backing.

3 When dry, glue the pin back onto the half-shell, positioned slightly more toward the top than at dead-center.

Materials

- 40mm x 30mm shell cabochon
- 60mm x 50mm half-shell
- 5 grams purple iris 11º seed beads (A)
- 2 grams bronze 11º seed beads (B)
- 3 grams purple iris 8º seed beads (C)
- 1 gram black 14º seed beads (D)
- 1 gram bronze 14º seed beads (E)
- 20 bronze 3mm round faceted beads (F)
- 10 bronze 4mm round faceted beads (G)
- 10 purple iris 8mm x 6mm teardrop beads (H)
- Gem glue
- 1" pin back
- 2 2½" squares black leather
- Black Nymo B or D thread
- Size 10 or 12 beading needle

119

Bead Key

A
B
C
D
E
F
G
H

Crystal Point Necklace

For centuries, crystals have been prized for their mystical qualities. They have been used in jewelry for just as long. When choosing a crystal to bead around, look for one that is larger at the top, preferably with a piece that sticks out and acts as a natural barrier to keep the beading from sliding. This one was held easily with a band around and one across the top.

For the center:

1 Referring to the Peyote stitch instructions on pages 22 and 23, use crystal 14º seed beads to make a ring long enough to go around the upper part of the crystal. Tie the ends of thread in a knot. This ring will become your first two rows. Do tubular Peyote weave with the lavender 14º seed beads for three rows and finish the band with two more rows of crystal 14º seed beads.

2 Use crystal 14º seed beads to weave a Peyote strap two beads wide to go snugly over the top of the crystal. Keep the weave as tight as you can. Attach this strap to the first band.

3 Use crystal 14º seed beads to weave another Peyote strap four beads wide and long enough so that there is approximately ⅛" gap between the center of the strap and the top of the crystal. Attach it from one side of the first band to the other side to create the pendant hanger.

For the fringe:

1 Bring the needle through one of the crystal seed beads at the bottom of the first band and string on one crystal 14º seed bead and two lavender 14º seed beads. Repeat bead sequence (B-A-A) four more times.

2 String on one crystal 14º seed bead, one crystal 8º seed bead, and one lavender 14º seed bead.

3 Bring the thread around and pass the needle back through the crystal 8º seed bead and up through the rest of the strand.

4 Repeat steps 1 through 3 two more times, for a total of three fringe strands. Do one strand with a bead pattern of A-A-A-B repeated four times. End with A-C-A. For third strand A-A-A-A-A-B repeated twice. End with one C and one A.

For the neck strap:

1 Thread the needle with about 2 yards of thread and string on a crimp bead. Place the other end of thread in a second needle and pass both needles through a clamshell bead tip from the inside out. Close the clamshell tip.

2 Pass both needles through one lavender 14º seed bead, one crystal 14º seed bead, and one lavender 14º seed bead.

3 Separate the threads.

4 Referring to the right-angle weave instructions on pages 18-20, use the crystal and lavender 14º seed beads to create a strand pattern like that in Figure 10-5 and approximately 20" long.

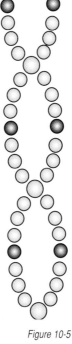

Figure 10-5

5 At the other end, pass both threads through one lavender 14º seed bead, one crystal 14º seed bead, and one lavender 14º seed bead.

6 End with a clamshell tip and a crimp bead.

7 Use jump rings to attach the clasp to each clamshell tip.

Materials

- Quartz crystal
- 10 grams lavender luster 14º seed beads (A)
- 10 grams crystal aurora borealis 14º seed beads (B)
- 1 gram crystal aurora borealis 11º seed beads (C)
- 4 crystal aurora borealis 8º seed beads (D)
- Gold toggle clasp
- 2 gold clamshell bead tips
- 2 gold jump rings
- 2 small crimp beads
- White Nymo B thread
- Size 12 beading needle

Bead Key

- A
- B
- C
- D

121

Leather Pouch Necklace

The ghost beads used in this project were purchased on the
Navajo Reservation. The wooden beads are actually piñon seeds
that grow on pine trees. When dried, they are used extensively
as beads on Navajo beaded pieces. When fresh, they are edible.
The beads are a nice addition to the bone and turquoise used on
this leather pouch.

1 Single-thread your needle with as much thread as you can handle and bring the needle from the back to the front of the upper corner of the flap, about ¼" from the edge.

2 String on beads in the sequence shown in Figure 10-6 (E-E-E-B-E-A-E-B-E-D-E-E-E-E-C-E-E-E). This is the fetish fringe.

Figure 10-6 (fetish fringe)

3 Pass the thread back through the first two of the four silver seed beads strung after the bone fetish and continue back up through the rest of the beads on the strand. Pass through the flap in the same hole you first came up through.

4 Bring the needle up through the pouch flap about ¼" away from the first fringe.

5 The next fringe is created with the bead sequence shown in Figure 10-7 (E-E-E-B-E-A-E-B-E-E-E-E-C-E-E-E). This is a regular fringe (no fetish).

Figure 10-7 (regular fringe)

6 Continue making fringe in a pattern of one fetish fringe followed by three regular fringe until you reach the other corner of the flap. Tie and cut off the thread end.

7 With a new thread length, make several fringe strands on the strap where the pouch meets it on one side. These fringe are essentially repeats of those created in steps 2 and 3, but you should vary the lengths, either by adding or subtracting beads. Tie and cut off the thread end.

8 Attach the bone figure to the flap by bringing the needle up through the back of the pouch, with the idea of centering the figure.

9 String on approximately 18 silver seed beads, position the bone figure in place so the beads will go around the neck, and push the needle back through the pouch. Tie and cut off the thread end.

Materials

- Leather pouch with long strap
- 23 piñon seed beads (A)
- 40 small turquoise nuggets (B)
- 20 brown 15mm x 5mm dagger beads (C)
- 9 bone fetishes (D)
- 300 silver 11° seed beads (E)
- Carved bone figure
- Gray braided filament line
- Size 10 beading needle

Bead Key

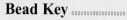

A
B
C
D
E

123

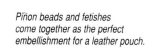

Piñon beads and fetishes come together as the perfect embellishment for a leather pouch.

For the holiday season, try beading around a bright red Christmas tree bulb for a festive pendant. What makes this piece of netting different is the use of #1 bugle beads for the sections.

On a trip to Oregon many years ago, I found this lovely sawed shell in a gift shop along the coast. I made a necklace of various fibers for it and wore it like that for several years. Then, it layed around unworn for a long time. When I learned how to make this shell-like Dutch spiral chain, it gave my pendant new life.

Janet Flynn's lovely bracelet features a Mabe' pearl as the focal point. The pearl is incorporated using Peyote stitch.

My mother-in-law collected marbles all her life. Her collection was made up only of marbles she found—and she had a large jar full. When she sold her home, she sold her collection as well. I chose a few of them before the sale to make into a necklace for her.

The clasp of this necklace is an antique faceted glass button that has been cabochan bead-set. It hides a magnetic clasp that joins the ends of the beaded chain. The nacklace was supposed to be longer, but I ran out of the matte black beads. I did not follow my own advice to always buy more beads than you think you will need for a project.

I teach a class to beginners on how to make a miniature beaded ornament. Because I can't resist making jewelry out of whatever I find, I fancied my ornament up and put it on a beaded chain.

RESOURCES

Beads

Morning Light Emporium
P.O. Box 92
Paonia, CO 81428
Phone: (800) 392-0365
Web site: www.mlebeads.com

Wild Things
21771 Sky High Boulevard
Pine Grove, CA 95665
Phone: (209) 296-8447
Web site: www.wildthingsbeads.com

Crystals

Azotic Coating Technology, Inc.
921 37th Avenue NW
Rochester, MN 55901
Phone: (507) 280-6763
Web site: www.azotic.us

Glues

Beacon Adhesives
124 Mac Questen Parkway South
Mount Vernon, NY 10550
Phone: (914) 699-3400
Web site: www.beacon1.com

Findings and Stringing Wires

Beadalon
Wire and Cable Specialties
205 Carter Drive
West Chester, PA 19382
Phone: (866) 423-2325
Web site: www.beadalon.com

Gemstone Cabochons

One-of-a-Kind Rock Shop
Highway 76 Strip #2855
Branson, MO 65616
Phone: (877) 331-0011
Web site: www.1ofaknd.com

Dichroic Glass Cabochons

Dema Designs
P.O. Box 577467
Modesto, CA 95357-7467
Phone: (209) 985-5033
Web site: www.demadesigns.com

Glass Stamping Supplies

Making Tracks, Ink.
P.O. Box 7486
Kalispell, MT 59904
Phone: (406) 755-6211
Web site: www.makingtracksink.com

Restoration Hardware

Van Dykes Restorers
P.O. Box 278
39771 S.D. Highway 34
Woonsocket, SD 57385
Phone: (605) 796-4425 or (800) 558-1234
Web site: www.vandykes.com

CONTRIBUTORS

Ella Johnson-Bentley (Moods in Stones Brooches) is a national beading instructor whose work has been featured in other beading books. Ella resides in Juneau, Alaska.

Berrie Butrick (Scalloped Peyote and Cabochon Necklace) is from Garretsville, Ohio. She teaches in Ohio and every winter in Quartzsite, Arizona. Contact her at: www.beads-n-rocks.com.

Elisa Cossey (Jasper Cabochon Necklace) is a published and accomplished beader. She is also a certified PMC instructor and a glass artist. She resides in rural Oklahoma.

Linda Currier (Peyote Barrels Necklace) of Elsie Creations is a bead artist and instructor. She teaches at national shows and bead shops close to her home in Faribault, Minnesota.

Cheryl Erickson (Princess Sandra Mae) is a professional bead artist and national instructor from West Des Moines, Iowa. Her work has been featured in books, galleries, and national tours. Contact her at: www.beadsbycheryl.com.

Erika Faust (Beaded Fish Lure Necklaces) of Leavering, Michigan, travels throughout her state doing art shows, festivals, and workshops hoping to inspire others to explore the fascinating world of beads.

Myrna Fligg (Tea Infuser Necklace) is an avid beader and member of LHF Bead Group and the Iowa Bead Society. She lives in Clive, Iowa.

Janet Flynn (Mabe's Pearl Bracelet) is a nurse and textbook author from Great Falls, Virginia. She teaches at national bead shows and can be reached at: www.janetflynn.com.

D.J. Levine (Doughnut Ties) of Manitou Springs, Colorado, is a member of the Rocky Mountain Bead Society. She has been beading since 1986, after seeing old Native American beadwork.

Stella Maris (Matchbox Necklace) is a bead and wire artist who lives and works on a yacht in Fort Lauderdale, Florida. She often raids the engine room of the yacht looking for unusual items to use in her jewelry.

Betty Oliver (Dichroic Glass Necklace) and her husband have a booth at Quartzsite every winter and sell beading and Dichroic glass cabochons. They live in Daniel, Wyoming.

Sigrid Wynn Evans (Beaded Doll Brooches) of The Beaded Bear in Modesto, California, is the author of numerous books on beading. She is a frequent contributor to the popular beading magazines.

ABOUT THE
AUTHOR

Drawing on her art education degree from Drake University, Carole Rodgers began her second art career by designing cross stitch for magazine articles. Finding her talents to be in demand, she then expanded into numerous other needlework and crafts disciplines, including beading.

Carole soon found herself designing 150 to 200 original projects per year for magazines, books, kits, and project sheets. To date, she is the author/designer of 99 pattern leaflets and hundreds of magazine articles and holds five patents for new product development.

Carole teaches beading and needlework classes and also serves as a consultant to manufacturers in the craft industry. She has been actively involved in promoting crafts, beading, and needlework in professional organizations and on craft television programs.

Although well-trained in numerous media, Carole admits her first love is beading. She has yet to find a beading technique that she doesn't like and is always on the lookout for new ones she hasn't tried. Her love of combining unusual items with beads led to the writing of this book.

Carole's beads go with her when traveling with her husband, LeRoy, in their fifth-wheel trailer. They attend numerous bead and trade shows and have recently started selling at some of them. (LeRoy just purchased a bigger truck so they would have more room to haul beads!)

Carole is a member of the Iowa Bead Society, LHF Bead Group, Hobby Industry Association, Society of Crafts Designers, and Embroiderer's Guild of America.

The Rodgers presently live on the family farm in south central Iowa.